American Romances

American Romances

Essays by
Rebecca Brown

City Lights Books
San Francisco, CA

Cover design by em dash
Interior design by Linda Ronan

ACKNOWLEDGMENTS

The author wishes to thank the editors of the periodicals and anthologies in
which many of these pieces have appeared in these or other forms: *Arcade,
Ellipses, Experimental Theology, Foodlore, The Richard Hugo House Literary
Series, Monkey Puzzle* (Japan), the *Stranger, Suspect Thoughts* and *Detroit:
Telegraph* (Museum of Contemporary Art, Detroit). Also, thanks to Cot-
tages at Hedgebrook and Centrum for residencies in 2007 and 2008.

Library of Congress Cataloging-in-Publication Data
Brown, Rebecca.
American romances : essays / Rebecca Brown.
    p. cm.
ISBN 978-0-87286-498-6
I. Title.
PS3552.R6973A44 2009
814'.54—dc22

                        2008035716

Visit our web site: www.citylights.com

City Lights Books are published at the City Lights Bookstore,
261 Columbus Avenue, San Francisco, CA 94133

Contents

Hawthorne   9

A Child of Her Time   31

The Priests   51

God without Words   67

Extreme Reading   83

Invisible   97

My Western   131

Young Goodman Brown: A Gloss   157

When a writer calls his work a romance, it need hardly be observed that he wishes to claim certain latitude, both as to its fashion and material, which he would not have felt himself entitled to assume had he professed to be writing a novel. The latter form of composition is presumed to aim at a very minute fidelity, not merely to the possible, but to the probable and ordinary course of man's experience. The former—while, as a work of art, it must rigidly subject itself to laws, and while it sins unpardonably so far as it may swerve aside from the truth of the human heart—has fairly a right to present that truth under circumstances, to a great extent, of the writer's own choosing or creation.

—Nathaniel Hawthorne, Preface to
The House of the Seven Gables

There is something in this native land business
and you cannot get away from it.
—Gertrude Stein, Wars I Have Seen

Hawthorne

a) Nathaniel, American author (1804–1864).

b) California suburb where Brian Wilson, American composer and Beach Boy (1942–), was raised.

Oh, the sins of the fathers! Oh, the visitations upon the sons! The dream of America! The nightmare, the horror, the hope.

The Puritans dreamt of the City on the Hill and came to the New World to build it.[1] Then when it went to hell their sons and sons of sons went west, and daughters, too. Go West, Young Man! Get away if you can! Get out before the city you built upon the hill implodes and takes you with it! Go West, Young Boy! The future's there! And beaches, too! Your Destiny and ours, both Manifest and otherwise, are way out west, far out, in the place the sun goes down each day and dies.

And so, to California they went, eventually to Hawthorne, suburb of the City of Angels. It was as far as they could go because then the land runs out, the only thing beyond is water, which no one can, unless they're Jesus, walk on, but they tried (on surfboards) and to some degree they could, but then they couldn't.

Because as much as anyone tries to ride a wave, a wave can't last forever. No surf stays up for good. It crashes or it comes ashore. It's soaked up by the sand, sucked down to earth, then further down, as they both say and sing, to hell and back again.

They set out with their modest, pure, angelic wives and found on the other coast the tanned and leggy, long-haired girls, perditious daughters of their bedeviled dreams. The Goodwives of Plymouth, Massachusetts, who covered the vanity of hair and clothed themselves in abstentious garb had mostly been obedient, Anne Hutchinson not-withstanding.[2] Though she was a deviant, wasn't she? Iniquitous. But way out west their malefactress daughters uncovered, grew, then cut their hair (Where did their long hair go?), the sons grew theirs, and everyone removed their sober clothes. Their children and their children's kids who'd been spared not the rod, were scruffy, unwashed, drugged and had an awful lot of sex. (See Manson, Charles, friend of brother Dennis, drummer, the cute one.) The daughters who'd been silent, pure (of, like, or as a Puritan) reported they'd had concourse with the Evil One who'd come to them in bodily form, sent by those they accused. They called these others witches (hippies, commies, terrorists) and they were stoned. They threw them in the water and they drowned. Like surfers who aren't strong enough, or are, except when some great, unexpected wave, a giant maw as big as the whale that got Gepetto although without a wooden puppet come to rescue, swallows them.

How deep is the ocean?

Enough to drown us all.

Nathaniel Hawthorne's great-however-many-grandfather, William Hathorne (note no "w" in the old man's name; we'll get to that later), was among the first Puritans to emigrate to New England in 1630.[3] His westward move was made in a ship, and it wasn't easy. There was all of that sickness and puking and death. That leaving behind and forgetting and not forgetting. All of that forever goodbye and never return and always wonder. William Hathorne first settled in Dorchester (Why did they name new places after old places they had left? Because no matter how much you want to, you never unbecome the place you came from), Massachusetts. He only stayed a while and then he moved to Salem where he thrived. Nathaniel Hawthorne, in "The Custom House," the introductory chapter to *The Scarlet Letter*, describes "[t]he figure of that first ancestor" as "grave, bearded, sable-cloaked, [a] steeple-crowned progenitor ... with his Bible and his sword ... soldier, legislator, judge; he was a ruler in the Church, he had all the Puritanical traits, both good and evil. He was likewise a bitter persecutor."[4] This William became deputy to the General Court of Massachusetts, speaker of the house, commissioner to the board of the United Colonies of New England and a renowned Indian Fighter (read: Genocider. For "Thou shalt not kill" did not apply to subhumans, which, though they were the ones who welcomed them and fed them, helped them stay alive, was how our forebears regarded the people who were already living on this continent). William Hathorne also was a judge and, in keeping with the Puritan justice his people had suffered in England but then brought with them because no matter how much you want to you can never unbecome the thing you are, meted out harsh punishments against evildoers such as: cutting off ears; boring holes in women's tongues with red-hot irons; starvation; dragging naked women through the streets while having them flailed by a constable with a cord-knotted whip, thus drawing blood, the desired result known as "stripes" (as in Isaiah, which the Bible-quoting Puritans would know, though we, godless and godforsaken souls, if we know it at all, probably picked it up from Handel's *Messiah*: "and with his stripes we are he-e-e-e-e-e-e-e-e-e-e-e-e-e-e-a-led"). The gallows. Putting into stocks. The pillory. Thumbscrews. Shackles (metal fastenings, usually a linked pair for the wrists, ankles, or both. See also: fetter, manacle. Also, any thing that keeps one from acting, thinking or developing as one desires. Remember them). Public humiliation such as having to walk around with the name of your crime written on a board hanging from your neck, and the board, being also very heavy, leaving marks on your neck and shoulders when—that is, if—you get to take it off. Drowning. (If she floats she's a witch, if she's innocent she drowns. There's water enough for all of us.) Stoning. Stretching on a rack, ripping off toe- and/or fingernails, ridicule, scorn, water boarding, throwing feces on, threatening with dogs, blinding with black hoods, prodding with electric prods, pissing on their holy books, making them do humiliating sexual things with themselves and with each other while photographing them and photographing ourselves making them do these things, thumbs up, hamming it up, grinning for the camera—

Wait a second. They didn't do *all* of those things back then, did they? Electricity hadn't been invented yet, nor photography. They only did *some* of those things. The other things had to wait until, through rational inquiry and scientific progress, we invented them.

Did I just call that progress?

The Puritans of seventeenth-century America branded them, that is, the people they punished. Not themselves. What I mean is, yes, they did brand themselves in the sense of branding fellow members of their towns, villages, communities who were evildoers, but they (Oh dear, this "they" and "them" business can get confusing. Sometimes you can't tell who you are or the others are, who's us, who's them, as if in some weird way we [they?] are the same, which isn't the case. Or is it?)

did not brand themselves through personal choice for artistic reasons, as our young people do today, decorating themselves artfully, as is also done with piercings, tattoos, scarification, collars, chains around the neck while playing "slave" and so forth. The Puritans didn't do that. The collars and chains our forebears (and to be fair, not all of them; some of them were abolitionists) put around others' necks were not for the purpose of costuming and/or stating a preference or proclivity. The others around whose necks they put these things were not in what we call "mutually consensual" relationships: they were slaves.

Likewise, the branding the Puritans enjoyed was not the personally chosen but rather the imposed-by-others variety, such as burning the letter "B" on a burglar's forehead.

Not a big leap from there to the scarlet letter "A" emblazoned on a woman's chest.

While being branded, by the way, one's brain, heart, back, forehead, neck, or what you will, fries, sizzles, bubbles, burns, blisters and/ or bleeds or what it will. One might try to think oneself away but one cannot turn away. They've seen to that. Though maybe if one is lucky, one might black out and not remember much. Though we've already established, haven't we, that one can never forget what happened to one, the place from whence one came, because it stays inside us, in our DNA, a kind of body/moral memory?

On the other hand, you might, if (or before) you black out, see stars.

Are those the stars and stripes we hear so much about forever?

God only knows.

Brian Wilson's grandfather William "Buddy" Wilson headed back to California in 1914.[5] (What is it with these grandfathers, Nathaniel's and Brian's both, named William? I guess it's a common enough name, my brother's for example. Not my father's, though, who was Virgil, and who, despite being a man with troubling qualities, was a decent enough guy to not saddle a boy with a name like his. As for our father's difficult qualities, my brother is more the expert on that than I.) I said William Wilson went "back to" California because when he was young, he, William ("Buddy"), had gone to California with his father, also William (Brian's great-grandfather?), who tried, in 1904, to move the family from Kansas to California in search of a better life that did not transpire, so the Wilsons returned to the midwest where William pere, not William "Buddy," resumed work as a plumber and then later William (son? pere?) came back. See what I mean about how everyone gets confused with everyone else? Like we're all sort of the same person trying the same things and making the same mistakes again and again and again?

Edgar Allan Poe, a contemporary of Nathaniel Hawthorne, wrote a story called "William Wilson." Actually, he wrote "William Wilson" twice, once in 1839 and then a variation in 1845. Even a fictional William Wilson gets mixed up with other versions of himself! It gets worse. "William Wilson" ends like this: "In me didst thou exist—and, in my death, see by this image, which is thine own, how utterly thou hast murdered thyself."[6]

I am you who destroyed yourself. Your dream will be the death of all your kids.

William Wilson went back to California in 1914. He was ambitious, determined, stocky, and a drinker often to the point of violence. He beat his family, particularly his wife. Sometimes his son, Murry, tried to rescue his mother, coming between her and his father, who then hit him, so then he hit his father back, and so on and so forth.

When he grew up, Murry Wilson, Brian's father, was, like his father Buddy (William), ambitious, determined, stocky and, after he married (Audree Korthof in 1938) and became a father, a drinker often to the point of violence. Not against his wife, though, just his sons. His sons were Brian (born 1942: composer, arranger, producer, dreamer, genius); Dennis (1944: the drummer, the cute one, the sexy one, the one who fought back most, the one who drowned); and Carl (1946: the quiet one, the chubby one, the lead guitar who took over producing the band when Brian dropped out in the late '60s when he went crazy. Dead of cancer in 1998).

Murry had work during the Depression, when a lot of other people didn't, and he was proud of that. He always said if you worked hard enough you would succeed in America. His sons remember him shouting, over and over again, and in the vernacular, the Puritan work ethic upon which this great nation was founded: "You've got to get in there and kick ass!" Murry moved up the ranks at the Southern California Gas Company to a post in junior administration. After his sons were born and World War II ended, he moved his family to Hawthorne.

It was a move up. He got a better job in administration at Good-year Tire Rubber Company where, in a perhaps Nathaniel-Haw-thorne-not-on-a-good-day, metaphor-like accident, he lost his left eye. (Blind. No perspective. Can't see past the nose on his face, etc.) Murry left Goodyear (though his sons stayed in its shadow for a while, writing song after song about cars, car tires, burning rubber: "gotta be cool now, power shift here we go"[7]) to start his own business. He called it A. B. L. E. (Always Better Lasting Equipment), a name the Puritans could have dreamt up, as if a divine prescription for the perfectibility of God's chosen children always getting better, as if someday, in some New! Improved! beyond we would be better and forever lasting.

Though Murry pushed his boys, often literally, to get what they wanted, as soon as they started getting it, he resented them. Demeaned them. Then he tried to control both what they got and them.

For what Murry had always wanted, ever since he was a boy, was to write hit songs.

But Puritans don't sing and dance. To do so is to sin.

The dreams of fathers visit sons; the failures and the jealousies as well.

William Hathorne's son, John, became, in 1683, a deputy to the General Court in Boston. I don't know if this was before or after 34-year-old John married a 14-year-old girl, their notions of evildoing being somewhat different from ours. (Poor Jerry Lee Lewis! To think he might have fared better as a Puritan!) Anyway, John Hathorne (still no "w" in his name), Nathaniel's grandfather, "inherited," in Nathaniel's ("The Custom House") words, "the prosecuting spirit, and made himself so conspicuous in the martyrdom of the witches, that their blood may fairly be said to have left a stain upon him," and, we may conclude with confidence, upon his descendants. For Nathaniel went on to confess, "I, the present writer, as their representative, hereby take shame upon myself for their sakes, and pray that any curse incurred by them—as I have heard, and as the dreary and unprosperous condition of the race for many a long year back, would argue to exist—may now and henceforth be removed."

John Hathorne certainly could have been cursed, having dispensed most gruesome punishments such as—Oh Christ, let's not go through all that again; see above, if you must—to persons of all ages. This Hathorne was the one who, during the trials of 1692, condemned the Salem witches to the gallows and to drown.

Fulfill your father's dreams and he will envy you to death.
You take your father's sins upon yourself.

A century and some years later, while living at his family home in Salem, Nathaniel Hathorne walked, reclusive and alone, to Gallows Hill, to be among the ghosts of those his ancestors condemned.

Can you remember things you didn't do but someone else did? Can you get over them for someone else? Can you get over them at all? Can you forgive them?

What if they're not forgivable?

The Scarlet Letter: A Romance, published in 1850, was mostly written in 1849, the year of the California Gold Rush. As contemporaries of his were heading west again, where they hoped this time to find, if not a spiritual, at least a financial paradise, Nathaniel Hawthorne was looking back at what his forebears had done wrong.

The Scarlet Letter was Hawthorne's fourth book for adults (he'd also written for kids) and, after the middling successes of his earlier work, he was surprised it did as well as it did.[8] The first edition of 2,500 copies sold out in ten days and his publishers had to reprint. In other words, this story of forbidden love was a hit.

In the chapter entitled "The Recognition," Hester Prynne, condemned to wear the scarlet letter "A" on her dress, is leaving prison with her newborn love child ("Never meant to be!"). Someone, Hawthorne narrates, "the eldest clergyman of Boston, a great scholar," calls "Hearken unto me, Hester Prynne!" and exhorts her to confess, repent and name the father of her child. This speaker is, like many characters in Hawthorne's work, based on a real person, in this case a leading Puritan divine, John Wilson (1591–1667).

Look, I'm not saying this Wilson was an ancestor of our California-bound Wilsons. On the other hand, don't we all believe, as our Puritan ancestors did, that if we go back far enough, we all go back to the same old Adam and Eve?

Brian remembers hearing "Rhapsody in Blue" on a record player when he was two, and loving it.

Murry remembers, sometime before Brian was one, carrying his baby on his shoulders and singing, and Brian imitating perfectly the song: "I just fell in love with him," he says.

Brian and his brothers sang each other to sleep at night, their three-part harmony angelic, sweet, divine. Their father stood outside their bedroom door and listened, misty-eyed.

He later beat them.

Hawthorne's father died at sea when he was four. After that, his sister Elizabeth recalled, Nathaniel loved to read. She remembers her six-year-old brother sitting in a corner pretending to read his dead father's copy of *Pilgrim's Progress*.

Brian said he went deaf in one ear when his father beat him.
Half of what he hears he only hears inside his head.
But then he said elsewhere that he was born that way.

No matter who tells the story, the story changes.

Nathaniel hurt his foot when he was nine, in 1813 and, incapacitated, read even more. He walked with a limp, self-consciously. He wrote both to reveal and to hide. From "The Custom House":

It is scarcely decorous . . . to speak at all, even where we speak impersonally. . . . thoughts are often frozen and utterance benumbed ... we may prate of the circumstances that lie around us, and even of ourself, but still keep the inmost Me behind its veil.

Half of what he said he only said inside his head.

Though it didn't appear on an album until 1963, the first ballad Brian ever wrote, "Surfer Girl," was inspired by "When You Wish Upon a Star," the song Jiminy Cricket sings to the wooden toy who wants to be a boy, Pinocchio. He composed this song while driving in a car on Hawthorne Boulevard.

After his father died the family moved down a social rung, and Nathaniel and his mother and sisters moved into his mother's family's many-gabled home. They paid rent and board, and were polite, impermanent and nervous hangers-on.

He was a child set apart, an oddity, a troubled boy inside a room inside a seven-gabled house.

Murry bought a professional-quality organ so he and Audree could play duets. Though Brian played piano and listened to records, Murry taunted him: No discipline. A jackass. Lazy.

Nathaniel's father turned his back on the traditional professions of the Hathorne men (judges, soldiers, murderers) by going to sea, and died when he was young. How could Nathaniel not turn his back too?

Because everyone is confused with everyone else. Everyone's sort of the same person making the same mistakes again. Not getting and not getting over it. Not better, though lasting forever, alas.

When he was 14, Brian went to Hawthorne High. He was tall, fun-loving, sweet and a fantastic baseball player. He began spending time at his buddies' houses listening to records and the radio, and getting away from Murry.

When he was 16, Nathaniel started a family newspaper called the *Spectator*, which he always was, looking in from the outside.

When he was 16, Brian was singing his own arrangements of the Four Freshman, Bill Haley and Elvis, with friends at school and with brothers and cousins at family gatherings.

Nathaniel went to Bowdoin College because it was near where some relatives lived in Maine and was inexpensive. There, though he became friends with future president Franklin Pierce and a lifelong, cigar-smoking Democrat, he was loath to study anything that would lead to a conventional profession.

Brian went to Hawthorne High where he gave his first quasi-public performance, an adaptation of "Hully Gully" turned into a campaign song for a friend who was running for student government. After Hawthorne High, Brian went to El Camino Junior College where he studied music and psychology until he dropped out because one day his little brother Dennis came home talking about surfing and Brian decided to write a song about that. A few weekends later, the Wilson parents went to Mexico for a holiday and left the boys with money for food. The brothers and their folk-singing friend, Al Jardine, spent this money, and some lent to them by Al's mom, on renting a mic, an amp and a standup bass. Then, with cousin Mike Love, they spent the weekend rehearsing "Surfin'" in hopes of making a demo tape. When Murry came home, he yelled at them for having spent the money the way they had. They begged him to listen to the song, and when he heard it he thought that they might have a hit and promptly appointed himself the manager of the Wilson family band. At first they were called "The Pendeltons," after the striped shirts the boys wore.

Nathaniel Hawthorne was a natty dresser.

Murry worked hard to cultivate publishing and radio contacts for the band, but he also humiliated and fought with his sons, more physically with Dennis and psychologically, in the studio, with Brian. In 1965 the sons had to fire their father from the band.

I'm bugged at my ol' man
'cause he's makin' me stay in my own room.
Darn my dad . . .

I wish I could see outside
but he's tacked up boards on my window . . .
Gosh it's dark . . .

—"I'm Bugged At My Ol' Man" (Brian Wilson,
from *Summer Days and Summer Nights*)

The Beach Boys could not, however, fire their father from being their father.

Nathaniel tried to. When he was 21, he changed the spelling of his surname, adding the "w." As if with this single letter he could separate himself from them. As if a single letter, as if a "B" branded on a burglar's face, a scarlet "A" across a woman's breast, could tell us who you are.

Brian wrote a string of hits. He was the native genius, American music's answer to the sophisticated pop of the British Invasion.

While Paul Revere and the Raiders could spoof, with their tights and Colonial-Era-looking jackets, a rebuff of the English, they ended up the butts of jokes. (Remember their *Midnight Ride?*[9]) Brian and the California sound he created not only rivaled the Beatles, Animals and Stones (who, after all, had created their sound by imitating American blues and rockabilly) on the charts, he also gained the admiration of classical composers like Leonard Bernstein. Everyone wanted to work with Brian Wilson in the studio. He treated the studio as an instrument.

Nathaniel's books were a string of hits, much-read and well-reviewed. He was revered at a time his countrymen were trying to create a particularly American culture (The Hudson River painters, Melville, Whitman, Poe), distinct from the English and European models they'd been handed. He treated his own, his family's and our nation's history as Romance. A story we cannot escape. A myth that will not ever have an end.

He saw himself as set apart, an oddity, a wounded boy inside a room, a gabled house, a continent of sons and daughters doomed.

Gosh, it's dark.

Brian Wilson kept to his house for years. After the triumph of *Pet Sounds* (1966), he pulled the plug on what would have been his masterpiece, *Smile*, and lay in bed. He took a lot of drugs and ate a lot of hamburgers, ignored his wife and daughters and got fat. Sometimes in bed or at his piano and in his filthy pajamas, he wrote little songs about health food, feeling great and love. When he did leave his home, he wandered, long-haired, filthy-bearded, unwashed, weird. Everyone thought he was crazy.

Nathaniel Hawthorne kept to his house for years. After graduating from Bowdoin, he returned to ghost-filled Salem, to live in his family home. (Melville later called him "Mr. Noble Melancholy.") He wrote in isolation and published his first novel anonymously (there was something about his father's name that galled him) and at his own expense. Around this time he also added the "w" to his name. He soon pulled the plug on his own career by burning every copy of the novel he could find. For the next ten or so years, he lived reclusively with his mother and sisters, stayed in his room and wrote, tore up what he wrote, and published, anonymously, little stories. When he walked to the graves of people who'd been murdered by his Hathorne forbears, he walked alone. He was evasive, skittish, melancholy, weird. Everyone thought he was crazy.

But maybe it was the world that was crazy then. Mid-century America was not only the land of transcendentalism but also of Transcendental Meditation, of spiritualism and the Jesus movement, of mesmerism and the Manson Family, Ouija boards and table rapping, good vibrations and animal magnetism. Millennial cults and Back to the Land-ers, the California Gold Rush and the Summer of Love, of railroads and rocket ships, Seneca Falls and *Ms.* magazine, the Civil War and civil rights, assassinations of presidents, and Edgar Allan Poe.

He wrote *The Scarlet Letter* the year of the California Gold Rush. He wrote "The Warmth of the Sun" after the assassination of Kennedy. An elegy, a fantasy. A warning, a regret.

He lived beside and walked along the shore of the Atlantic, the Pacific, but couldn't keep his sights out there alone. He looked back where he had come from and toward the waves his fathers rode, the waves his brothers tried to ride. He walked among the graves his fathers and his brothers filled.

He was an innocent, an always-boy. A skeptic, never-boy. Forever wise, forever sad. Forever wanting to forgive and to pretend it wasn't bad and getting worse. Forever going back as if remembering or taking on, undoing what the fathers did, the fathers' sins, our own. He was before and past and utterly of his time.

In 1969 he wrote, or rather cowrote, a song:

Time will not wait for me
Time is my destiny . . .

I can break away from that lonely life
and do what I wanna do
my world is new

Where the shackles that have held me down
I'm gonna make way for each happy day.

> —from "Break Away" (B. Wilson - R. Dunbar)

For Hawthorne time was always past and destiny. We are always looking back. What happened? Why? We came from there. How do we get away? Forgive or be forgiven? His words were his attempts to break away.

Brian Wilson stayed an innocent. For him time is, as it is for all westward travelers, the future.[10] In the future you can start over again. Despite the "shackles" (remember them?) that held him as they held his Puritan forebears. But he still hopes, as if one can, "my world is new."

As if the fathers' sins can wash away.

The happy "Break Away" song was credited to Brian and a collaborator named Reggie Dunbar. Reggie Dunbar was a pseudonym used by Murry, Brian's father.

A son forgives a father's sins.

What mercy has the child for the man.

NOTES

1 John Winthrop, who sailed to the Massachusetts Bay area in 1630 with a group of Puritans, wrote this about their mission to set up a home in the New World: "For wee must Consider that we shall be as a Citty upon a Hill, the eies of all people are upon us." Also, that God would make of them "a story and a by-word through the world." In other words, "wee" came here already rarin' to go with the assignment of being storytellers hired by God to perform, for the clueless primitives in the rest of the backward world, how to behave. Winthrop is quoted (p. 11) by the great writer on Puritanism, Perry Miller, in his great book about Puritans, *Errand into the Wilderness* (Harper Torchbooks, 1964), the first footnote of which (p. vii) is: "American scholarship is prone to idealize the footnote."

2 When Anne Hutchinson first began holding meetings at her home for other female Puritans of the Massachusetts Bay Colony, the guys didn't mind. But when she and her lady friends began to disagree with the male leaders on matters such as warfare (Men: Let's kill the Indians; Women: Let's not), original sin (Men: Eve did it; Women: No, she didn't), and their own intelligence (Men: Women shouldn't talk in church; Women: Yes, we should), her Puritan elders (all male) brought her to trial for dissension, witchcraft and lustfulness. She was found guilty and banished. Now there is a statue of her in front of the Massachusetts State House. She's looking heavenward. See *Divine Rebel: The Life of Anne Marbury Hutchinson*, by Selma R. Williams (Holt Rinehart and Winston, 1981).

3 On Hawthorne: *The Scarlet Letter and Other Tales of the Puritans*, edited by Harry Levin (Houghton Mifflin/Riverside Edition, 1961), and *A Historical Guide to Nathaniel Hawthorne*, Larry J. Reynolds, ed. (Oxford University Press, 2001), in particular the essay by Brenda Wineapple. I also consulted Wineapple's full-length biography, *Hawthorne: A Life* (Knopf, 2003), which is tremendous.

4 My copy of *The Scarlet Letter Letter and Other Tales of the Puritans*, with the great intro by Harry Levin, has a lot of fab, creepy stuff about the Puritans. It's also where I got many of Hawthorne's quotations about Romances, etc., that appear in this book.

5 My main sources for the Brian Wilson/Beach Boys material were: *Catch a Wave: The Rise, Fall and Redemption of the Beach Boys' Brian Wilson*, by Peter Ames Carlin (Rodale, 2006) and *Wouldn't It Be Nice: My Own Story*, by Brian Wilson and Todd Gold (HarperCollins, 1991), a signed copy of which I found on the bookshelf in the brown house where Chris and Donna and Dave and George and Aldo and I stayed when we went to Hawaii to celebrate the end of Donna's chemo. It was like an endless summer. We sat on a patio Brian Wilson had sat on. We cooked in a kitchen Brian Wilson ate food from. We had pillow fights in a bed Brian Wilson slept in. We swam from a rock Brian Wilson swam from. I'm glad we did and can remember, because now Donna is dead.

6 Edgar Allan Poe, *The Fall of the House of Usher and Other Writings*, David Galloway, ed. (Penguin, 1986).

Bonus Trivia Fun Fact Question: What do Puritan John (or was it William?) Hathorne, rockabilly hero Jerry Lee Lewis and Edgar Allan Poe all have in common?

Answer: They each married their 14-year-old cousins! (Maybe it was 13. But you get my drift.)

7 Brian wrote most of the Beach Boys music and someone else wrote most of the lyrics. The liner notes to the Capitol Records reissues detail who did what where, including lyricists such as Gary Usher, Terry Melcher (son of Doris Day!), the icky Mike Love, and for a while, early in his solo career, the highly disturbing Eugene Landy.

David Leaf, the Beach Boys' and Brian Wilson's chief biographer (see *The Beach Boys and the California Myth* [Grosset & Dunlap, 1978]) wrote many of those liner notes.

The great Beach Boys lyrics, though, are/were mostly courtesy of the glorious Van Dyke Parks, particularly on *Smile*, 1967 and 2004. Parks also does his own terrific stuff (music and lyrics), such as *Orange Crate Art* and *Song Cycle*, and reappears on Brian Wilson's 2008 *That Lucky Old Sun*. Thank you, Van Dyke Parks. You, sir, are a great American.

8 In addition to writing generally about the homeland of his forefathers, Hawthorne also wrote about specific homes in which he lived. *Mosses from an Old Manse*, his collection of tales from 1846, was named after and mostly written in the "Old Manse" Hawthorne and his wife Sophia rented in Concord. The house in *The House of the Seven Gables* (1851) was modeled closely on the house young Nathaniel had to move to with his mother and sister after his father died. Both of these books contain stories of houses that are haunted by history and secrecy and memory and ghosts and ancient books.

9 *Midnight Ride* (1966) was Paul Revere and the Raider's second album, after their 1965 debut, *Just Like Me*. On the cover of *Midnight Ride* Paul Revere, Mark Lindsay, et al. are sitting inside a dark stone house holding candles ("One if by Land, Two if by Sea") and looking apprehensive about the British invasion(s, both the first guns-and-shooting one and the second twist-and-shouting one).

10 I live out west, though not in California where I was born, but I get back east from time to time to work and visit friends and to wallow around in history, such as when I go to see my writer friend Dawn Paul and we go to see Hawthorne stuff. We went to the Old Manse, where Hawthorne lived with pictures of a bunch of old guys on the walls upstairs, and to the House of the Seven Gables where I bought the refrigerator magnet, the Christmas ornament, the coloring books, the postcards and the eraser, and walked to the gravesides and cemeteries of old Salem and on the beach, as Nathaniel Hawthorne also did.

Nathaniel Hawthorne was a beach boy too.

It can hardly be told whether it is a joy or a pain after such a momentary vision to gaze around in the broad daylight of reality.

—Nathaniel Hawthorne, "The Old Manse"

In many dark old tomes she met with chapters full of romance and poetry.

—Nathaniel Hawthorne, "The Birthmark"

A Child of Her Time

I think I was nostalgic as a child.[1] Even before I knew that word, I had this sense that the best was already over with.

I remember once when I was little—I don't remember exactly how old—my sister and I were given matching baby dolls for Christmas. They weren't fancy, the way some of the dolls they were starting to make in those days were. They didn't talk if you pulled a string or wet themselves if you put water in their mouths. Their arms and legs didn't move, and their eyes didn't open and close, and they weren't the size of real, actual babies. They were *dolls*—maybe six or eight inches long, of soft, beige plastic with painted-on eyes and hair, brown for my sister's, blonde for mine.

What I do remember is how I felt when we got the dolls. I loved the fact that my sister's and my dolls were not fancy, that our mother was acting as if these simple dolls would be enough for us. I loved, but was also sad, that as matching dolls—they both had flower-patterned dresses on, one yellow and one blue—they were meant to suggest a closeness between my sister and me that we had never had.

I knew kids who dressed in matching clothes and I also knew that unless there was something wrong with them, they would not keep doing that when they were older. There was something about being little that allowed that, but whatever that thing was, it would go away when you grew up. Something would happen and one day you wouldn't want to be like your brother or sister or anyone in your family.

My sister is seven years older than me, and if she was still young enough to have been given a baby doll, she couldn't have been more than nine or ten, which would have made me two or three. And while she liked playing with dolls, she did not like being paired with me. I didn't like playing with dolls that much, but I remember wanting my sister and me to play with those dolls together so that our mother would be happy.

My mother had read the Laura Ingalls Wilder books to us, and there was that part when their grandfather or somebody brought the kids oranges for Christmas. The kids were thrilled with the oranges. They didn't know whether to eat them immediately or to save them. We, on the other hand, had oranges all the time in Florida, and nothing any of us had meant half as much as those oranges did to the Laura Ingalls Wilder kids.[2]

I don't remember ever playing with those poor dolls together, but now, after years of hating how she treated me when I was a child, I can look back and sympathize with my sister. When she was born, my sister was her mother's only child, her princess, her adored. My father was not around for the birth, but when he did finally see his firstborn he was proud. Like most men in the '40s and '50s, he didn't know what to do with a baby, and watched in awe as his pretty young wife took care of it. Then, as was his pattern for years, he went back out on navy tour again. When he came home on leave, my mother met him eagerly, excited to see him and show him the growing baby. Most of my mother's time was spent without him, and most of my sister's first year of life she had our mother to herself. Then, about a year after my sister, my brother came along. With his second child, my father was less puzzled. After the kid grew up a bit, he'd be able to do boy things with him like hunting and fishing. Though my sister was still her mother's little girl, she was no longer her only child. She'd been supplanted.

My father's visits home were special occasions. He'd talk to his wife about exotic, foreign places he'd been, with names like Tripoli and Lisbon, Cartagena. He talked of minarets and palaces, gondolas and the Alps, and said someday he'd take her there. She said she hoped he would. His wife cooked him his favorite food and talked about the kids: how they were sleeping through the night, then walking, talking, potty trained. She talked about the house: how she had rigged a clothesline when the dryer broke, and fixed a leaky sink.

One of the things my father had to learn in the navy was photography, and to finish his course he had to make a portfolio. Some of the men shot photos of the wilderness or airplanes, sports. My father shot photos of his wife and kids and put them in an album that my mother kept for years. In the pictures, my mother's skin is smooth, and her hair is long and dark. In the one particular photo I am thinking of, my brother and sister are sitting on the couch on either side of her and our mother is reading to them. They're all engrossed, their faces bent over the book open in her lap. My sister is wearing a plaid dress with an apron and anklets, my brother a shirt and shorts and sandals. Neither of the children's legs reaches the floor. All three of their mouths and cheeks are smeared with licorice—they all loved licorice, even the black kind—but they seem happily unaware of their messes. In this picture, my father regards his children and his pretty wife with love.

After several years of this, his touring with the navy took its toll. My siblings grew up knowing their father as a visitor. Though my mother missed her husband at first, she grew used to his being gone, adapted to raising her kids alone, to being a woman without a man. Then when my father did come home, he came as an intruder.

How soon after my father took that picture of his wife and his children on the couch did he start resenting them? When did he begin to feel his wife had turned from being a woman who adored him into a mother who only adored her children? When did my father begin to feel, as my sister would, that he had been supplanted?

When did my mother begin to feel that her husband cared more for his job, his country, than for his family? When did she begin to resent his expectation that his visits home were special occasions, that he came home "on vacation" and to hunt and fish with his Navy pals, while she, vacation-less, maintained the home and family? When did each begin to feel the other had betrayed them?

By the time I was born, a year or two after the licorice photo, my parents had pushed each other as far away as they could while still staying in a marriage. Their good years were behind them, they were only biding time.

Did I somehow know this as a baby, then a child? Was knowing this the "cause" of my nostalgia?

I felt responsible for the dolls and for my mother, as if I knew that I, that we, her children had taken her husband from her, and that she was only staying married to him for us, and in particular for the youngest child, me. Did I somehow want to fix for her the mess I had created by being born? Did I somehow reason that whatever happiness she might still have had something to do with some old idea she once had had of what a family was, how children were? And that the last place this idea could manifest was me?

I'm assuming there was some kind of "reasoning" in what I did or felt, but I don't know that. I look for causes in retrospect but I bet at the time I didn't think like that at all.

I started off this essay by saying I didn't remember how old I was when I got that doll and then I tried to work that out. But if I don't remember something as simple as how old I was, how can I remember what I thought?

Because another time when I visited her, and my mother and I were shopping—I don't remember where—for some snacks to take on a hike and I said, "How about some licorice," she said, "I can't stand licorice." I said, "You used to love it," and she said no, she never liked it. "But what about the picture," I said, "the one with you and Bill and Betty on the couch, that Dad took. Your mouth is smeared with it." "No," my mother laughed, "You kids and your father loved it, but I've always hated licorice." We went back and forth like this in the car on the way home and then when we got back to her apartment she got out the photo and there it was, exactly *not* as I had remembered it. My brother's and sister's faces are smeared, but my mother's is perfectly clean.

"See?" she said.

But even now when I think of that picture, at first I see my mother's face smeared with licorice. Then I have to remember what she told me, and what I saw in the photo when I looked again, but I still don't see it right inside my head. I remember, or something, despite what I know is true, something that never was.

I said I didn't remember exactly how old I was when I got that doll. I also don't remember how old I was when I stopped believing in Santa. I do remember it was on a Christmas Day when I found, on one of the presents Santa was supposed to have left beneath our Christmas tree, a price tag. The present was a shooting gallery my mother would have gotten in an attempt to find me something in which our father might have interest. The shooting gallery was cardboard, in a box cut out like a theater set, and attached by springs to the stage part on the bottom were four cardboard ducks. The one with the most colors, I knew from what my father had told me about their markings, was a wood duck. There was also a mallard drake (shiny green head, purple flash on the side) and a hen (brown) and, I think, a teal (teal). You were supposed to shoot the ducks with the enclosed gun, which had darts with rubber suckers on the end that were supposed to, but didn't, stick to the ducks when you hit them. I found the price tag on the back of the box.

I hope I didn't act, when I showed my mother the price tag, as if I didn't know what it meant. I hope I didn't ask something designed to make me appear sweet and innocent like, "Did Santa forget to take off the price tag?" I think I suspected, even then, that my mother had purposely left the price tag on so that our family could finally admit that the Santa story we'd kept pretending we believed for one another was finally over.

I say I don't remember exactly when I stopped believing in Santa, but I remember the room I found the present in. It was the living room of our first house in Spain, and we were only in that house a year. We moved to Spain after the navy finally gave my father a posting where he could live at home. Though of course by the time he got this job, the possibility of him having a life at "home" was almost nil. I think my parents hoped this posting, which would allow his family to share his life in an exotic foreign place, might turn the marriage around.

He worked downtown in Madrid mostly, but also on the navy base. When he worked downtown, my father came home for lunch the way the Spaniards did. When we were new to Spain my mother, who had rarely left her native Oklahoma and never been abroad before, was keen on taking advantage of the learning opportunities afforded by being in a foreign culture. So, in addition to allowing us to go to bullfights, which she herself only went to once, she signed me up for flamenco lessons. My brother and sister, who were in high school and old enough to protest, didn't have to do anything like that. They were adamant about staying as American as possible—my sister in her bobby socks and penny loafers, my brother in his short-sleeved madras shirts and blue jeans.

My flamenco teacher, a young, taut, dark-eyed, olive-skinned and scantily dressed dancer, came to our house to give me lessons. She came midday, when my father was home for lunch, and gave me my lesson in the living room while my father watched from where he ate. Despite my parents' encouragement, my lessons did not last. I was terrible at all of it—holding my hands in a curve and my feet straight as splints. I was also very bad at castanets.

Anyway, I remember those lessons were in the same room where in December of that year we all stopped pretending we believed in Santa Claus, and also the same room we had all been in the November night our neighbor came to tell us that the president had been shot.

We didn't believe him. Our neighbor, Mr. Bosch, was, according to my father, an embarrassment who could not hold his liquor. Mr. Bosch was also a Catholic and my father, who had always hated Kennedy—for his Catholic-ness, his northern accent, his youthfulness, his politics and his hair—assumed that the teary-eyed Mr. Bosch was just shouting about some maudlin Catholic thing. My father walked the drunken, distraught Mr. Bosch around the block a couple of times then back to his house to sleep it off. But by the time my father came back to us, we were hearing on the radio—we didn't have a TV then— that the president had been shot, and we had to believe it.

Of course I didn't understand all that the shooting meant. I doubt if any of us did. My father, even if he hated Kennedy, was a career military man who believed in the U.S. government and that it always could and would take care of its own. My brother and sister, who were starting to listen to music my father hated, believed the young, good-looking president with a not-bad haircut and a beautiful wife was going to make the world a cooler place. My mother, who'd idolized F.D.R., and still thought that the president, any president, was somehow above the rest of us, was devastated that a mere criminal could murder him.

Was this an end of childhood for all of us?

We came back to the states in '66. My father served out a couple more years in the military, but then they piped him over.[3] He floundered around at civilian life and the marriage finally ended. When my parents finally split in 1969, they were the first people any of us knew who got divorced. Back then if you were married, you were supposed to pretend you were happy, but I also know they stayed married because they didn't want to have failed—at love, at family, at doing what you were supposed to do. Plus, there were practical reasons. Though my mother had gone to college and taught grade school, raising three kids on one income would have been tough. In any event, they waited to get divorced until my brother and sister went off to college and I was in junior high.

By that time the sexual revolution and the feminist movement were underway, and my brother and sister were flower children and taking drugs, and M.L.K. and R.F.K. and Malcolm X had been murdered. But unlike when the president was shot, we saw these things immediately ourselves, the pictures in the papers and the clips on our TV: the black men on the motel porch pointing to where the bullets came from, Sirhan Sirhan in handcuffs and the body bags from Vietnam.

We saw these things ourselves this time and knew that everybody else was seeing them too. Everyone knew that things had changed and no one was a child anymore.[4]

NOTES

1 "The Puritan's faith began with a primitive kind of nostalgia." Kai T. Erikson, *Wayward Puritans: A Study in the Sociology of Deviance* (John Wiley & Sons, Inc., 1966), p. 47.

From my *Webster's New World Dictionary* (2nd concise edition, 1982): **nos.tal.gia** n. [Modl. <Gr.*Nostos*, a return + ALGIA).

1. A longing for home; homesickness.
2. A longing for something far away or of former times.

and

al.gia *a noun-forming suffix meaning* pain.

The pain of returning returns
but you cannot
the pain of leaving what you left
and knowing what you wanted never was.

2 I recently went back to find that place where Laura Ingalls Wilder talks about the kids getting oranges for Christmas and being so thrilled. In the first book of the series, *Little House in the Big Woods*, originally published in 1931, I found this:

> Mary was bigger than Laura, and she had a rag doll named Nettie. Laura had only a corncob wrapped in a handkerchief, but it was a good doll. It was named Susan. It wasn't Susan's fault that she was only a corncob. Sometimes Mary let Laura hold Nettie, but she did it only when Susan couldn't see.

I was nostalgic for somebody else's childhood.

I reread the Christmas chapter and saw that it wasn't an orange each child got, but something even smaller, a single peppermint stick. I thought of my brother's and sister's and my stockings crammed with chocolate bars and SweeTarts and those paper tubes of flavored, colored powder, and that we always wanted more. The Ingalls kids, unlike us, were "so happy they could hardly speak at first ... just looked with shiny eyes." Each child was also given a pair of bright red mittens. If we got mittens—which were not toys—we pouted. And if they were matching ones, so you and your siblings would look alike, that was embarrassing.

When Laura did, finally, get her own rag doll ("so beautiful that Laura could not say a word"), the other kids weren't jealous, they were glad for her.

What was wrong with us? When had we turned so greedy?

Little House in the Big Woods ends after Laura and her sister have been put to bed. Their father is playing his fiddle and singing "Auld Lang Syne" to his tucked-in girls:

> Laura called out softly, "What are the days of auld syne, Pa?"
>
> "They are the days of a long time ago, Laura," Pa said. "Go to sleep now."
>
> But Laura lay awake a while, listening to Pa's fiddle softly playing to the lonely sound of the wind in the Big Woods. She looked at Pa sitting on the bench by the hearth, the fire-light gleaming on his brown hair and beard and glistening on the honey-brown fiddle. She looked at Ma, gently rocking and knitting.
>
> She thought to herself, "This is now."
>
> She was glad that the cozy house and Pa and Ma and the fire-light and the music, were now. They could not be forgotten, she thought, because now is now. It can never be a long time ago.
>
> (*Little House in the Big Woods*, HarperTrophy, 1971, pp. 237–238)

The author who had been that girl had maybe not forgotten, but those of us born after her had never known. We weren't like children used to be, but selfish, petty, mean. To us the thought of "long ago" was hokey.

But maybe Ingalls Wilder's insistence ("not forgotten ... now is now. . . . It can never be long ago.") was less the truth than something of a wish.

Laura Ingalls Wilder (1867–1957) had been writing newspaper columns for years. After her mother died in 1924 and her sister in 1928, she began, in grief, to write her memories. It was not until after the market crashed in 1929 that she sought advice from her savvy author daughter, Rose, about what to do with these memoirs. The degree to which Rose edited, rewrote or added to her mother's first-person accounts is debatable. What is clear is that Rose recognized that her mother's story would appeal to poor, Depression-era Americans who longed for a more innocent time. Plus, if they could sell them, they might make back the dough they'd lost in the collapse.

3 "Piped over" is when they get rid of you from the military because you can't stay at the rank you are forever but they aren't going to give you a raise because you're a mess. Or at least this is how I was given to understand it later. What I remember is going to the base somewhere, into an airplane hangar, and my father was there in his dress whites and a couple of other navy men and my mother and me, and then the sound of the whistle like they have on ship, and it was over.

My brother remembers this differently, although it may be he remembers another time entirely. What my brother remembers is a ceremony and my father being given a medal for something, but he does not remember what. Are my brother and I remembering two different events or just different versions of the same event? Both of us know we remember poorly.

4   So when was anyone ever a child?
    Or ever a child like then?

The child we remember is a child we invent
to tell us who we thought we were,
or wanted to have been.

In 1850, a decade or so before the childhood that Laura Ingalls Wilder would remember so idyllically, Hawthorne described a very different one.

It belonged to a girl named Pearl born in the 1660s, the offspring of an unmarried scarlet-letter-wearing woman and a Puritan minister. She was her mother's living sign of sin, her father's guilty shame.

Hawthorne was the father of two when he conceived of Pearl. His eldest daughter was born in 1844, and the 40-year-old struggling author and his wife, Sophia, named their child, in homage to Spenser's *Faerie Queen*, Una. No wonder she was strange. Sometimes her father didn't quite know what to make of her:

> There is something that almost frightens me about the child—I know not whether elfish or angelic, but, at all events, supernatural. She steps so boldly into the midst of everything, shrinks from nothing, has such a comprehension of everything, seems at times to have but little delicacy, and anon shows that she possesses the finest essence of it; now so hard, now so tender; now so perfectly unreasonable, soon again so wise. In short, I now and then catch an aspect of her, in which I cannot believe her to be my own human child, but a spirit strangely mingled with good and evil, haunting the house where I dwell.
>
> (Nathaniel Hawthorne, *The American Notebooks*, ed. Randall Stewart, Yale University Press, 1933, pp. 210–211)

Is any parent's kid their own? Are children not the human beings we come from?

Una was five when her unemployed father, having lost his job at the Custom House, began to write what would become *The Scarlet Letter*.

The "Pearl" chapter describes

"[a] little creature, whose innocent life had sprung ... out of the rank luxuriance of a guilty passion." (p. 88)

(Rank. Guilty.)

"Her Pearl!—For so had Hester called her.... 'Pearl,' as being of great price—purchased with all she had,—her mother's only treasure!" (p. 88)

(Her name is milky pink and white, a shimmered thing made from an irritant. She was her mother's everything and cost her mother all.)

"Day after day, [the mother] looked fearfully into the child's expanding nature; ever dreading to detect some dark and wild peculiarity that should correspond with the guiltiness to which she owed her being.... The child could not be made amenable to rules." (pp. 88–89)

("There is something that almost frightens me ..."

The child will become how she was born. Her parents and their culture were disobedient; they left their parents' land and law as if a new God spoke to them, replacing all the old rules.)

"An imp of evil, emblem and product of sin ... she had no right among christened infants." (p. 92)

("I know not whether elfish or angelic."

As if the christened are not evil, both the products and means of making sin.)

"She saw the children of the settlement ... disporting themselves in such grim fashion as the Puritanic nurture would permit; playing at going to church, perchance, or at scourging Quakers; or taking scalpels in a sham-fight with the Indians; or scaring one another with freaks of imitating witchcraft. Pearl ... never sought to make acquaintance. If spoken to, she would not speak again." (p. 93)

(What Christian, rule-abiding, godly children did was scourge, scalpel, fight and scare.)

"Pearl ... amused herself with gathering handfuls of wildflowers, and flinging them, one by one, at her mother's bosom; dancing up and down, like a little elf, whenever she hit the scarlet letter. Hester's first motion had been to cover her bosom with her clasped hands.... Still came the battery of flowers ... covering her mother's breast with hurts for which she could find no balm in this world." p. 96)

(What child would use a flower as a weapon?)

"'Child, what are thou?' cried the mother.

'O, I am your little Pearl!' answered the child ...

... Pearl laughed and began to dance up and down, with the humorsome gesticulation of a little imp, whose next freak might be to fly up the chimney.

'Tell me, then, what thou are, and who sent thee hither? ... Thy Heavenly Father sent thee!' ...

'He did not send me!' cried she, positively, 'I have no Heavenly Father!'" (p. 97)

(No earthly father claims her. She is her earthly mother's scar, her heavenly father's fallen rebel.

The child written in America is a bastard.)

Maybe Pearl's spookiness was too much for even "Mr. Noble Melancholy." For after *The Scarlet Letter*, Hawthorne turned as far from a child such as Pearl and the Puritan world that made her as one could get. In 1852, the author, who had had two more children by then, wrote a book for kids. *A Wonder-Book for Boys and Girls* (Ticknor, Reed and Fields, 1852) retold myths of ancient Greece. Instead of a dim, depressed Puritan Reverend Dimmesdale, the young male at the center of this book is a sparkling 18-year-old student, Eustace Bright. Hawthorne named the child characters, as he had named his second daughter, for flowers: "Primrose, Periwinkle, Sweet Fern, Dandelion, Blue Eye, Clover, Huckleberry Cowslip, Squash-Blossom, Milkweed, Plaintain and Buttercup." (p. 2)

If Puritan-made Pearl stood for a hardened whitish thing of great price made of greater pain, each child in *A Wonder-Book* stands for the opposite—a humble, living, prettily colored flower. As Hawthorne grew into fatherhood he wanted to create, in words, a sweeter tale of childhood, if only from the very, very far away and very long ago.

But impish Pearl was prescient, an early version of the bastards, misfits, runaways, orphans, rebels and battered kids we would imagine as and for ourselves:

1868: Louis May Alcott publishes *Little Women*, which tells a story, loosely based, as Ingalls Wilder's was, on her own life. While their father is absent, the girl children run the house. The Louisa May stand-in is Jo, a tomboy who likes "boy's games, and work, and manners," and declares, "I can't get over my disappointment in not being a boy." "I'm the man of the family, now that papa is away," Jo says. A gender misfit only too happy to replace her absent dad.

1884: Mark Twain, long after the river transport culture he had loved so in his youth was obsolete, tries to bring it back in *The Adventures of Huckleberry Finn*. Huck's mother is gone, his father is a drunk. At least he has a friend in Jim and he is good to him. (The country isn't. Jim is black, therefore a slave.) The white boy is a juvenile delinquent running from the authorities. (Hawthorne called his Huckleberry in *A Wonder-Book* "a mischievous little elf.")

1900 (which promised to begin the American century!): L. Frank Baum publishes the first of his *Wizard of Oz* books. Dorothy is made homeless by a storm (no FEMA then), and then befriended by the brainless, heartless and cowardly. The city she relocates to is inhabited by midgets. She is the only one of her kind, a temporary orphan.

1903: *Babes in Toyland*, Victor Herbert's operetta, later made into a movie (1936, Laurel and Hardy as horrible child-men), then another (1961, a stacked Annette Funicello and a swishy Tommy Sands as "children"), then a book (1986), opened in New York. In it a creepy uncle tries to kill two kids whose parents are already dead, then tries to "marry" a little friend of theirs to get the children's fortunes. The kids get help, in an arty pre-postmodern way, from characters from earlier children's lit (Miss Muffett, Georgy Porgy, Simple Simon, etc.), and live to tell the tale in time for Christmas. There are tons and tons of presents (unlike Ingalls Wilder's Christmases) for these pseudo-kids who have been chased by icky men for sex and dough.

1924: Another orphan, Annie, appears in the New York *Daily News* accompanied by another creepy pseudo "daddy" (Warbucks).

1929: "Our Gang," which had been silent in the flicks, begins to speak. This gang is a gaggle of poor, scrappy street kids who have been abused by teachers, cops, the odd mean aunts and uncles, etc. and so they raise themselves, like wolves.

No wonder by the '30s the Ingalls Wilders were creating a childhood we could remember, or at least imagine, fondly.

In 1935 Shirley Temple starred as *The Littlest Rebel* (David Butler, director, based on a novel by Edward Peple), an ever-smiling—except when she was pouting adorably—little girl living in the South during the Civil War. Talk about imagination! While her well-mannered plantation-owning parents were kind and gracious to their happy Negroes, the Northerners were rude. The Littlest Rebel wasn't rude to Negroes, she was a friend to them! In fact one of the little Negro girls who lived on the plantation, in tidy nice quarters, even brought Shirley Temple a birthday present! Also, Shirley and Mr. Bojangles (Bill Robinson) sang and danced like two peas in a pod (children and Negroes being roughly equivalent in that world) to raise money to help get Shirley's rebel daddy out of jail where he had been wrongly imprisoned. Shirley and Mr. Bojangles even got to meet Mr. Lincoln! Who was well-mannered and gracious to the little girl and her Negro. And everyone lived happily ever after.

By the 1960s, both Negroes and children had stopped believing the pretty stories they had been told. Negroes became Black and children became youth and both knew they were not the way their parents had portrayed them. They determined to make a different world, unlike the one their parents had fucked up (not knowing, alas, their parents and their parents' parents' parents [etc.], had once thought they were doing that themselves). The children of the '60s—flower children—declared themselves a new nation, free from their parents' old, outdated, uptight, puritan values. They'd start a brand-new, better world—a commune on a hill—where everyone shared everything (including one another) and they would will an end to war. A daisy stuck into a gun could stop it. They would wear flowers in their hair, instead of army helmets.

But a flower, like any living thing, buds prettily, then blooms and fades and dies. So, too, the flower child.

Three centuries after Pearl flung that peculiar battery of blooms at Momma's breast, the last flower child died. The imp had turned into a sex toy of indeterminate and/or multiple orientation(s), and dressed in New Orleans bawdy-house attire (low-cut top, boobs almost showing; scarlet skirt; voluptuous strings of voodoo and other beads; pink ostrich feather; mussed-up hair). She smoked and drank and, in the picture, sprawls upon a tawdry love seat. She smiles out at us—no—not at us exactly, but someone beside us we can't see. Is it her madam? Or a client? Dad? A child she remembers or invents?

This is the cover of Janis Joplin's posthumous *Pearl* of 1970. A one-time flower child, outfitted as a whore, dies of an overdose of everything. The '60s were really over then, and no one was a flower- or any other kind of child anymore.

We see her forebear in her face: our Pearl.

Hawthorne's earthly children didn't have much better lives. When Una was fourteen and living with her family in Italy, she contracted malaria, then typhus. She sort of recovered, though never fully, remaining sickly for the rest of her life, which included a mental breakdown, a period in an asylum, and a stay in a convent where, at the age of 33, she died.

Even then poor Una did not rest. She was buried in England, where she'd been living with her mother, Sophia. For a century and a half their graves were kept up with donations from a religious group. Then, in 2005, after some wayward roots of the hawthorn tree that had been planted over them pushed up through the ground and busted the headstones, this group decided, rather than dig up and replant the bones in the same place, they would send them back home.

That's how, in 2006, shortly after Brian Wilson had been resurrected with the *Smile* tour, Una's and Sophia's bones were brought home from England and reburied in these United States next to Nathaniel.

The second child, Julian (as in Saint Julian Hospitaller, who embraced the leper; see Flaubert's *Three Tales*, 1877), was born in 1846. The boy whose father was an old friend of a president and a famous man of letters dropped out of Harvard, became an only middling successful writer (his most well-known book being a biography of his father), failed at his first marriage and was imprisoned for embezzlement.

The third child, Rose, whom Hawthorne called his "autumn flower," married an alcoholic and lost her only child early. Then, after this child's death, Rose, whose father had been driven by the ghosts of his Puritan ancestors, converted to the Roman Catholic Church. After her husband died, Rose, like her sister before her, entered a convent. As Mother Mary Alphonsa Lathrop, she founded the Dominican Sisters of Hawthorne, an order that has now been caring, like Saint Julian, for victims of cancer (which her father may have died of, my dad, too; my mother did, and Donna) for more than a century. A few years ago the name of Mother Alphonsa was put forth in Rome to begin the process of canonization.

The flower of her father's fall
is reborn as a saint to those
his ancestors reviled
the purer rose redeeming fathers' sins.

I was a youth of gay . . . temperament . . . wayward and fanciful.
— Nathaniel Hawthorne, "Passages from
a Relinquished Work"

In fairyland there is no measurement of time.
—Nathaniel Hawthorne, "The Old Manse"

The Priests

We used to play priest.

Whoever was the biggest would tell everyone to go to mass or you'd get in trouble. She'd have a towel and she'd wrap it around her shoulders and make it hang down in front like that thing I now know is called a "surplice" and make us kneel down in front of her as if we were at the altar and bend our heads and she'd touch us on our heads and say "the body of Christ" and give us a Necco wafer. She'd put it on our tongue and hover over us until we swallowed it. You were supposed to chew it but I didn't. I kept it on my tongue and let it soften, thicken, melt, slough apart from papery to gluey to sticky and soft, like frosting, but also gritty, like powder except wet, and that was when it really started to taste.

It tasted like vanilla.

Though only at first, because we used the vanilla first because it was white, beige actually, like it was in real life, whereas after we ran out of white it tasted like grape or cherry or chocolate or, finally, orange. It tasted even more when it was sliding, warm and slippery, down my throat.

She'd listen for you to swallow and watch the movement in your neck then put the Dixie cup of Kool-Aid or Hawaiian Punch or Tang to your lips and say, "the blood of Christ," and you'd feel this little pressure against your lips, the waxy edge of the Dixie cup, and she'd push a little toward your teeth, and you'd open your mouth and your head would go back and she'd tip the cup toward you and you'd drink.

The priest made up the rules. The priest told us what everything was, what everything meant, and all about sins. All sins were bad, but some were very bad.

The priest said there were other things, secret things and signs we weren't ready to know yet but might be someday. The signs would tell you who was who, the secret things to do.

A lot of us kneeled like this at first, then later only me.

She was always the priest; I never was.

Sometimes for the altar she'd pick the sidewalk, not the real sidewalk but that ridge of concrete where it goes up from the street to your yard. I had to put my knees on the concrete. The top parts of my knees could be on the grass with my feet turned up like the soles of my shoes were looking up at heaven. If I was wearing sneakers this wasn't so bad, but if I was in flip flops or sandals, the street felt awful, although I liked those feelings some.

I also felt the end of the towel, the tips of her "surplice"—or was it "chasuble?" Maybe I'm not remembering right. Oh, what have I forgotten!—swaying against my shoulder or head or along the back of my exposed, bent-over neck.

We only played outside like that in summer.

In the winter we were in the house, alone, her mother still at work, my father somewhere, and she'd tell me to put a cushion from the couch down on the floor and kneel and wait while she left the room—she was going to the sacristy to prepare—then came back with Communion.

At first she'd just step into the hall and, almost as soon as my head was bowed, come back and touch my head with her sticky hand and say "the body . . . the blood," etc.

Later, however, she took her time.

Did she go to the bathroom and look at herself? Did she comb her hair, again, in front of the mirror? Or call on the phone to one of her friends, a popular girl or a boy? Did she saunter off to 7/11 to buy a coke? Or go out back and throw the ball to their whining chained-up dog? I don't remember. But I do remember her doing that before it died, throwing the ball to the tied-up dog. She always threw it just a little out of reach.

The "real" priests, in the church, were men,
but that didn't stop her.
And it didn't stop me from believing in her
and in whatever it was we did.

Later it wasn't a Necco
and later it wasn't one.
Later it was two
with creme to hold them.

(Crème, American: a whitish fake food designed to pass for cream. Invented because it was cheaper and had a shelf life of millennia. It fell from favor during the natural food boom, but later was reclaimed by liberal-minded vegans, vegetarians and persons of lactose intolerance.)

Two crisp and dry but sweet and round, so that your tongue, if you ran it around them, could lick along the edge like a curious cat. The bottom and top, though separate, were two, were similar, alike, the same.

The two, that is, were *homo* (etymologically from the Greek for *same*), they were not *hetero* (etymologically from the Greek for *other, different*).

They were, that is, a sign.

The two were not alone, which priests, that is, "real" priests, the ones in church, were meant to be.

Although we wondered.

Real priests were supposed to be like Jesus, who was celibate.

Although we wondered.

For though He didn't procreate, He said "this is my body," and then he said it was "a temple." There was also all of that about the disciple whom He loved, who lay his head upon His breast, who stood at the foot of the cross and did the things the women did, like weep and mourn and grieve, whose name was John.

Of course we wondered.

We wondered about them, all of them,
We wondered about ourselves.
We wondered if there were others,
then who they were,
then how to find them.

We found us in our history
read secretly in signs.

By the eleventh and twelfth centuries, many Christians in southern France had come to despise the official Roman Catholic clergy as insensitive to the lives of regular people, excessively materialistic and disgustingly wealthy. At a time when peasants starved, priests and monks were pudgy and pink as pigs. They looked like little Neros, all ruddy-faced and mincing in their swishy robes and pointy, pretty shoes. Their teeth were dark with too much wine and their breathing stank of sausage, booze and boys. Despite all their babbling about purity, they were promiscuous. They slept with boys and women, too, and girls and with each other. Sometimes they called the other one the "wife."

No wonder, then, that when two idealistic young clerics on their way home from a pilgrimage to Rome encountered the excesses of the church in Montpellier, they set out to reform all of Christendom. Dominic, better known to us today as Saint Dominic, the founder of the Dominican order, and his long-time companion, Diego, began a program of scripture study, introduced a new austerity into the church, and even founded, in 1206, a religious school for girls.

Dominic and Diego were not, however, the only reform-minded believers running around the south of France at the time. Long before the two friends arrived, the Cathars (from Greek Katharoi, meaning "pure ones," a term related to Katharsis or Catharsis, meaning "purification"), were spreading their own anti-materialist gospel. Also known as Albigensians, because their twelfth- and thirteenth-century incarnation was centered near the town of Albi, the Cathars were a neo-Manichaean sect whose ideas may have been introduced to France by an unnamed woman from Italy. (Unless it's something cool or even great, in which case it's attributed to "anonymous," it's always the woman's fault.) Or via Eastern European trade routes.

Neo-Manichaean thought was inspired by the ancient dualistic religion of Mani, which was based on the idea that Good and Evil—

God and Satan—are two separate and equally powerful forces in continuous battle with one another, and that our struggle here on the earth is this battle of material Evil versus the immaterial Good—i.e., our bodies versus our non-bodies. Mani (b. 216 AD), it must be said, was from Persia (now Iran), an Eastern locale whose very existence, not to mention its sexually liberal practices, had troubled to the point of obsession, the West.

We have had it out for them for centuries.

In any event, for Cathars the worst thing in the world, the temptation you really had to watch out for, was procreative sex. It not only brought two bodies together, it also could lead to the creation of another evil, sinful, suffering, carnal, beautiful body.

In order to help save the poor souls drawn to the heterosexually married state, God, the Albigensians believed, created *parfaits* ("pure souls"). *Parfaits* were elite persons who, like Roman Catholic priests, neither married nor procreated. However, unlike Catholic priests, *parfaits* were encouraged to create a life with another human being who, in the interest of avoiding the temptation of procreative sex, was to be a person of the same or *homo* gender.

Parfaits led and taught the larger number of congregants or *croyants* ("believers") who did have heterosexually procreated families. Though *croyants* too, it was hoped, would participate, before they died, in the *consolamentum*, a form of baptism that would render them almost as pure as the pure *parfaits*.

Cathar thought may have been introduced to France via an unnamed Italian woman, or it may have come via Eastern European—including Bulgarian—trade routes. So when people incited by the church started harassing and then persecuting Cathars, one of the things they called them was "Bulgarians," transliterated into English as "buggers," which later meant men interested in sex with other men.

Ways in which Cathars were persecuted included being beaten up, run out of town, burned, bashed, called sissies, or worse, "women," and having sticks rammed up their asses, the latter a wry commentary on reputed Cathar practice.

In addition to renouncing heterosexual marriage and procreation, the Albigensians also forbade the eating of any form or product of the flesh, even in the symbolic form of wine-as-blood and wafer-as-flesh.

A doctrine that forbade the eating of animal products was difficult to impart to a nation of gourmands. Nonetheless, the Albigensian *parfaits* journeyed extensively to spread their gospel, traveling, as they later dwelt, in same-sex pairs: women with women, men with men, other with other.

Albigensian practice, unlike that of the Roman church, allowed women full participation, even as *parfaits*. In fact, one of the reasons Dominic founded that girls' school was because he didn't want to lose all the Roman Catholic females who wanted to do something with their lives besides make babies to the Cathars.

As is often the case with missionaries, the *parfaits* adapted rituals practiced by the people they wished to convert. In the Roman Catholic eucharistic supper, one man served many—kind of like the wealthy wife of an industrialist doling out soup at some feel-good social-service project—and the believer ate the flesh and drank the blood of a single person, Jesus. The Albigensians' sacred supper, on the other hand, was *shared*, two believers feeding each other. It was also two believers feeding two things, for the single wafer of flesh had become a happy pair and the water-wine had turned to creme that bound them. This sweeter meal required neither death nor cannibalism. Plus, you got chocolate.

When word got around about how tasty the Albigensian sacred meal was, people started showing up at their revival meetings less to learn about the pure life than to eat. Almost overnight the delicious biscuit(s and creme) became France's number one snack food!

France had no idea its favorite snack food was the sacred feast of an outlawed sect, it just knew it was scrumptious. Nor did the savvy Cathars tell the general public they couldn't eat their cookies. In fact they encouraged people to eat them, because how you ate the cookie could signal to other secret Cathars you were one of them. Then you could go with them, or they with you, and together you could enjoy your own communion.

After Saint Dominic, better known to us today as the founder of the Inquisition, got wind that his reforms were less popular than those of this truly popular religious movement, he further decided, in the way only a dog of God can, to deal with the Albigensians. (Dominic's followers were known as *Domini Cane*, Dogs of God, because they protected, like shepherds' hounds, their flock, but also, like rabid curs, went after different others with their fangs.)

The Albigensian Crusade became official in 1209 when Pope Innocent III, a swishy-robed, pointy-shoed, immaculately coifed and boy-attended pontiff who was obsessed with *vir cum viris* (Latin for males who copulate with males) and *femina cum feminis* (Latin for females who copulate with females; see also females who do not wear swishy robes or pointy shoes or have immaculate coifs or fuck boys), authorized the genocide of the Albigensians and anyone else they thought a bit suspicious. The first campaign was the siege of Beziers and it was a doozy. Refugees fleeing the crusaders, whose shock-and-awesome fame had gone before them, had holed up in the church of Saint Mary Magdalene (a whore). The holy warriors dragged the people out of the church and slaughtered them all—men, women, others (especially others), and children. Villagers were dragged behind horses, hatcheted, mutilated, used for target practice, fired from their teaching jobs, waterboarded and given electroshock treatment. When the Cistercian abbot Arnaud was asked how to tell Albigensians from Catholics, he answered, *Slay them all. God will know his own.* (Latin:

Caedite eos. Novit enim Dominus qui sunt eius.) After everyone was dead, they burned the city down.

When the Inquisition became official in 1229, many of the remaining Cathars went underground. All across everywhere witches, weirdos, perverts, darkies, commies, trannies, punks, panhandlers and occasionally even liberal democrats were burned at the stake. Also, buggers/fags. (From Latin *faggot* meaning little stick, kindling, the stuff they used to start the fire to burn people at the stake. Heretics, in fact, soon became identified with the faggots used to burn them. Some faggots [the men, not the sticks] who refused to stop being faggots [buggers] even embroidered symbolic faggots [the sticks not the men] into their garments in defiance as if they were saying, I know you're going to get me, but I'm not going to be closeted by you fucking Nazis. [See everyone who ever wore a yellow star, a scarlet "A", an HIV tattoo. See also Joan of Arc, later sainted, though earlier roasted, for the crime of transvestitism. Wait—that sounds like she was sainted for being a transvestite, which she wasn't. I mean she *was* sainted and she was a transvestite, but she was not sainted for *being* a transvestite. For being a transvestite she was burned at the stake like a faggot, with faggots. What she was sainted for was having visions that today would get her put away forever in a mental institution though at least in that case she wouldn't be homeless. Also, colloquially, a cigarette.]

Joan of Arc didn't smoke [cigarettes, I mean. Though she herself, that is, her body, smoked, that is, her flesh, hair, fingernails, bones, etc., produced smoke when she/it/they was/were roasted at the stake.] In prison Joan ate, before she died, smuggled in by true believers, girls who dressed like boys and others, at the risk of their own imprisonment, with them, with their tongues tonguing the ridges, their mouths licking off and sucking out the creme, her last supper.)

The stake-burning mega-trend was helped along by Thomas Aquinas's (1225–1274) declaration that homosexuality was one of the worst worst worst of the "sins against nature" (Latin: *peccata contra naturam*).

Whose nature?

Fortunately, not all of our forebears were burned at the stake eviscerated ripped apart by horses (their arms and legs having been tied to four different animals) crushed inside an iron maiden hanged pressed to the width of an envelope by stones thrown into the river to drown had their tongues cut out balls cut off twats mutilated sentenced to hard labor chemically castrated made to undergo aversion therapy or fired from the Boy Scouts. Fortunately, some of them were only stuck into ships' galleys and forced to work like slaves. (For actual slavery see American history.)

Some of them got to America.

Then some of them made us.

I don't mean "made us" in the carnal sense (though they did so, and happily, some). I mean "made us" by keeping the faith, by carrying on the way they did and dressing the way they did, by doing things they knew we'd recognize, though others wouldn't, by leaving us signs like bread crumbs in the woods that told us we were not the first and that we weren't alone. They kept our secret and passed it on in hopes someday we'd see.

Though the Albigensian movement was suppressed by the Crusades, believers continued to have faith and meet in secret. A look at the map of the south of France will reveal the lingering presence of Cathar culture in village names such as Queribus (Latin for "Queer Town"); Montsegur (Latin for "Mountain Man Town" or "Daddyville," a town still occupied by large hairy men and their cubs); Foix (Latin for "fag"), and so forth. Gertrude Stein, a *parfait*, and her *parfait* wife, Alice B. Toklas, lived in Perpignan for many years and hostessed American military boys who traveled to see them two by two, initiating them into the cuisine, culture and unnatural practices of the Cathars.

Toklas was also the early twentieth-century Keeper of the Recipe. Among Toklas's contributions to Cathar/Albigensian culture were her insistence on the purity of the cocoa and the addition of optional other ingredients for particularly visionary rituals of worship.

Stein, for her part, was not only the authoress of the modern version of the Albigensian Liturgy of the Supper, but also actually The Giver of the Name to the cookie that had remained heretofore, for reasons of security, unnamed. The brilliant linguistic play for which Stein is known can be seen in the variety of sources, puns and interpretations of the simple four-letter name she created:

From Latin *or* meaning gold, *re* meaning King and *o* meaning oh. Starting and ending with "O" the omega, the beginning as/is the end, the completion of the whole, the roundness of the world, the lifted belly, the shape of the mouth in ecstasy, whether erotic or cuisinic, middled by the injunction to "re-ad" my (that is, Stein's own) books, to re-ad the signs you see around you everywhere, to re-peat what bears re-peating, to re-peat with all the earnestness of love, over and over re-peating and re-peating until you get it right, but also not only toward any end but just because the re-peating is exciting, lovely and peaceful. To start with "Or", thereby acknowledging that everything is only and infinitely possible, an either/or, a maybe else.

Then further, ore, the mass from which you mine the streak, the seam of what is hidden, what you want, the richest, sweetest thing.

A nod to the Or-phic mysteries, which or-iginated with Orpheus, the Singer! Whose poems could charm the pants off one.

Our sustenance.

Stein also told us how to read the secret meanings of both The Parts and of The Ways.

The wafers being hard and two are boys. They rub each other up and get that creme. The creme sticks them together like they're married, like if you pulled them apart before their time it's sticky and wrong, little frosting tips poking up like peaks, them crying out on both sides, ripped apart. Or if one side gets all the creme, like "getting the girl," as they say in the other history, like when you get to marry her, the other one, the other side is brown-black mostly sort of bruised-looking because no matter how clean you lick it away or scrape it with your teeth, a teeny little bit of it, like snow that's melting into dirt, remains. Some of it has seeped into the inside of the biscuit and it will not be removed, no, never, it's a stain, it's like a person who cannot forget a way he was, the way he should have stayed.

The two are also a woman's thighs, and the creme between—oh, the creme between!—is heaven's invitation.

Oh, to approach the thighs of the madonna! So firm and dark and clutching. Clutching what there is within but waiting to be out, and clutches you and what you want and what you want to give, to get from her, what is inside, both her and you, the moist and white and opening.

Her darkness spliced by mystery! Her cloven self both opening unto and pouring out, the thing you bring, the thing that you desire.

The white of sap, the thick of creme, like mothering of milk.

The Manichean meeting of the Evil and the Good, of black and white, of dark and light. Inside and out, the hard and soft and dry and moist, the chocolate and vanilla: cookie(s) and creme.

The mystery of the three in one: the biscuit Father, biscuit Son, and creme-y center Ghost.

A secret writ in Braille that you read out with your tongue.

The way you opened it, then what you did, would tell you and your fellows who you were.

If you ate it fast or whole, a bite and a break and a chew like it was just a snack, then you were clueless. We knew you were not one of us, and we might then be careful what we would say or do around you.

The rest of us knew what to do and how to do it right.

If she slowly, slowly twists it nice and even, one hand beneath and turning clockwise, and the other hand above and turning counter, if she holds her hands both openly but firmly, if she takes her precious time, then cracks it open, opens them and waits. Then if she brings it to her face and looks, at it and then at you, then breathes in like the ocean or the sky, the whole outdoors, if she breathes in deep the it of it, then, with her tongue or with her teeth, begins to lick or scrape or press along the white, if she leaves tracks of tongue or tooth around, across or down, into the creme then to the chocolate, then she stops, then takes a moment, looks again, as if she's looking at the dawning of the world, as if she's looking at a miracle, then starts, as slow as before, then gradually unslowing . . . if she removes the creme by slow firm tooth- or tongue-ful, then, finally, when the creme is gone, her mouth is sweet, and something's moist and melting, warm, then slipping down her throat like oil, wine, some thing divine, and then hands you the other. . . . The chocolate is supple, bending, nearly limp. If then she puts one in her mouth and one in yours, and sucks or tongues or presses, nibbles, bites, you know that she is one of us, *parfait* and pure and yours.

NOTES

Some of the historic stuff—and all of it's true, with the obvious exceptions of what I invented because I fantasize—comes from:

Rictor Norton, *A History of Homophobia*, "4 Gay Heretics and Witches" 15 April 2002. http://rictornorton.co.uk/homopho4.htm

You can read a lot about the historic residue of the Cathars et al. in *Montaillou*, by Emmanuel Le Roy Ladurie. This book is based on records of a heresy trial in the south of France from 1319 to 1324.

The Catholic Encyclopedia is where I got the specifics about Dominic and Diego, Pope Innocent III, the Crusades, etc. But I've also been fascinated by Dominic and his Dogs for years, and, even since I was a kid, the Crusades. (See also my book *The Dogs: A Modern Bestiary*, City Lights, 1998.)

I began reading Stein in high school on the advice of a deliriously, to me, androgynous camp counselor. A few years later, my mother gave me Janet Hobhouse's biography of Stein, *Everybody Who Was Anybody* (Putnam, 1975) for Christmas and then I found *The Autobiography of Alice B. Toklas* at the library and then, in college, the poems and lectures and the Modern Library and Black Sparrow editions and I made a Sunday afternoon salon with my writer and musician and painter pals in the old brownstone where some of us lived.

Other stuff comes from recent American history and the backs of snack boxes.

The following pages will contain a picture of my vagrant life, intermixed with specimens, generally brief and slight, of that great mass of fiction to which I gave existence and which has vanished like cloud-shapes.

—Nathaniel Hawthorne, "Pages from a Relinquished Work"

God without Words

In an 1812 letter to a friend of a friend, Felix Mendelssohn wrote this about his *Songs without Words*:

> People usually complain that music is so ambiguous; that they are doubtful as to what they should think when they hear it, whereas everyone understands words. For me, it is just the reverse. And that is so not only for whole speeches, but for single words also: they too seem to me so ambiguous, so indefinite, so open to misunderstanding in comparison with real music which fills one's soul with a thousand better things than words. To me, the music I love does not express thoughts too indefinite to be put into words, but too definite . . .
>
> If you ask me what I thought (in connection with one or another of the "Songs without Words"), I must say: the song itself as it stands. If, with one or the other of them, I had a specific word or specific words in mind, I should not

like to give them these titles, because words do not mean the same to one person as they mean to another; only the song says the same thing, arouses the same feeling, in one person as in another—a feeling that, however, cannot be expressed in the same words.

Resignation, melancholy, praise of God, a fox hunt—these are words which everyone interprets differently. What is resignation to one person is melancholy to another; a third thinks of both as lifeless. For a man who loves hunting, the fox hunt and praise of God might well be equivalents; he would feel that the winding of horns was really and truly the right way to praise God. To us a fox hunt is merely a fox hunt, and no matter how much we discussed the matter, we would get nowhere. The word remains ambiguous; but in music we would understand one another rightly.[1]

I came across this quotation when I started listening to Mendelssohn and I wanted to learn more about him. I learned, through words, about Mendelssohn's mistrust of words. Talking about music isn't music. But it was only through words that I was able to understand something about how inaccurate Mendelssohn considered words to be in regard to his music.

Now when I listen to *Songs without Words*,[2] I am aware of how consciously "without words" these pieces for solo piano are. Words would get in the way of this music.

When I am really listening, even if I am listening to someone talk or sing or read, I am not listening to words. I become a wordless thing that does not think but rather absorbs, becomes. For a while I get to escape my thinking, worrying, word-fretting mess of a brain.

There's a line from the *Tao Te Ching*, the fourth-century Chinese book of wisdom: "One who knows does not speak; One who speaks does not know."[3]

There is some doubt about who Lao Tzu was, or exactly when he lived. In fact, the words "lao tzu" mean "old master" and it may be that the work is less the work of a single author than an anthology created by a series of "old masters." The One who spoke, that is to say, may not have been (only) One at all.

The more I really listen to Mendelssohn and Lao Tzu, the more I learn, I think, something about how hard it is for me, a being obsessed with words, to know God. Talking about God is not knowing God. The chattering, dithering, worrying back and forth I do in my head with words I have read about God, that other people have said about God, is not God.

Am I beginning to learn what saying isn't?

I don't know what to do with this. Actually, maybe I do know but I just don't want to do it. Because I'm afraid to stop studying and thinking and trying to understand about God in words and instead make room in my head, then maybe in the rest of me, for silence.

But I'm not good at understanding without words. I learn through words. My vocation is writing; my profession is teaching. Much of the sense I have made out of my life has been made with the help of words I have read or heard.

In the late 1960s, after my father, under somewhat mysterious circumstances, left the military, we moved to Arlington, Texas. My father had managed to get a job near Dallas in a plant that manufactured airplanes or airplane parts or something I never bothered to ask him about. This was the Vietnam era, and my brother and sister, just going off to college, and I, in seventh grade and the only one still living at home, were beginning, like a lot of people, to consider military guys, even ex-military guys, the enemy. My mother had considered my father the enemy for years.

Not long after my father got this job, he lost it, though my parents didn't tell me this for weeks. When I asked what my father was doing home all day nursing a bourbon in his big chair in front of the TV, they told me he was "on vacation." He moved out shortly afterwards, my parents got divorced, and I didn't see my father again for years.

There had been rumors about my father's behavior at work: that he didn't show up sometimes, that he was drunk and belligerent, that he had lied or was incompetent. I heard these rumors after he had left, from other kids whose fathers worked where my father had. I pretended I didn't care, but when I was by myself I went over and over in my head the words they'd said about my father.

After he left, I replaced my father in the big chair in front of the TV. Because I was at school, I couldn't watch during the day, but every night after my mother had gone to bed I watched the *Tonight Show*. Johnny Carson, I realized years later, looked and acted something like my father: handsome and wry and puckish. They had similar mannerisms—something about the way they laughed, a chuckle actually, nothing so vulgar as a guffaw—and they could both be suggestive without going overboard.

It took my mother several months to sell the only home that she and my father had ever owned, and when she did we moved across the highway to an apartment.

Arlington was different in some ways from places we had been when my father was in the military, but in some ways it was the same. It was different in that most people who were there had been there a long time and had cousins and second cousins who lived there, too. It was the same in that I was a new kid.

At Joe Bailey Junior High, home of the Fighting Rams, there were a lot of clubs: Music and Spanish and TARS ("Teens Aid Retarded Students"), Science and Pep Squad and Drama and Chess and Math. Different kinds of people were in these clubs: nerds in Science, smart in Honor Society, jocks in football, popular in Pep Squad, weird in Drama, Mexicans in Spanish, girls in French, etc. The biggest club in the school was God Squad. A lot of those kids were nice, quiet girls, but God Squad also had almost every kind of kid in it. It was an amazing thing—a miracle—that God Squad could bring together nerds and popular, jocks and "retardeds," and that everyone was nice to everyone else. At God Squad, people tried to be nice to everyone.

One of those nice girls kept inviting me to God Squad. I was starting to make friends with some smart kids so I didn't want to go, but this girl was so insistent, like she was trying really hard to make friends with me, so I finally said okay. This girl—was her name Nancy?—said she would come get me, but I didn't want her to come to my mother's and my apartment so I told her I'd meet her there. I walked across the highway to the meeting in a house in our old neighborhood.

My family had never gone to church much, only when our mother tried to take us so we could meet people. It would be some generic service at the military base with singing from our government-issued, pocket-sized New Testaments led by some officer's wife. But we never actually believed anything.

God Squad kids believed things. They knew that they were going to heaven and that, as they said frequently, "All things work for good for them that love the Lord." Also, that their Heavenly Father had numbered every hair of their heads and was always watching over them and would never, ever leave them. They had memorized all these Bible verses that sounded ancient and wise and had words like "thine" and "shalt" and "charity" and "He shall wipe away thy tears," and they knew stories about feeding the poor and healing the sick and things turning out all right. The God Squad kids said that all you had to do to be born again was accept in your heart and confess with your lips that Jesus Christ was your personal Lord and Savior.

Whereas if you did not accept Jesus Christ as your personal Lord and Savior you would go to hell.

At first I thought people who thought that were mean and stupid and also, with the whole "One Way" thing, arrogant. How could anyone really know those kinds of things? What about people in pagan countries, I asked, who never even heard of Jesus? Were they going to hell? Yes. Which is why we need to be missionaries. What about if people died when they were babies? Our ways are not God's ways, God's ways are not our ways, and sometimes we do not understand our Heavenly Father's will. What about Hitler, I asked. Could even Hitler be saved? If he accepted Jesus Christ as his personal Lord and Savior, yes, even Hitler could be saved.

I went over and over in my head the things about God Squad that I could not accept but I always kept coming back to the fact that the God Squad kids were really trying to be good, and God was helping them. Some of them, before they found Jesus, had been bad, as I learned when they gave their "witness."[4] Witnessing is when you tell your faith story. You tell it to be honest about your life as a sinner and also so that others might be inspired by the miracle God has worked in you. Some of the adult leaders of God Squad had been bad too. They had been adulterers or drunks or had no purpose to their lives or abandoned their kids. Then Jesus had saved them and they changed.

I didn't have some terrible thing like taking drugs or getting pregnant I needed saving from, but I loved that anyone could start over and be born again into the Christian family. So one day when I was at home alone in our apartment—I guess my mother was out—I knelt down by my bed and accepted in my heart and confessed with my lips that Jesus Christ was my personal Lord and Savior.

I didn't tell anyone at first. There's a place in the Bible—I can't tell you where it is now, but I'm sure back then I could have told you chapter and verse—that said to retreat to your closet to pray so you wouldn't be a showy hypocrite. I didn't want to be a showy hypocrite, but maybe I was a different kind. Maybe I didn't want to tell people, especially my new smart friends, about Jesus because I wasn't really a Christian but a fraud.

God Squad had shirts. On the days when your God Squad group was going to meet (there were groups all over town, all over the entire state), everyone in your group wore their shirt. They were Izod-style, short sleeved with collars, and they had GOD SQUAD and a cross over the pocket. I hadn't bought a God Squad shirt, not because I didn't want to spend money—I did give money for the poor and missionaries, etc. Did I not buy a shirt because it would identify me, the way a Girl Scout uniform would, as a member of a group I felt embarrassed, around some people, to be a part of?

After a while, like any new love, the initial excitement wore off and the little things that had bothered me a little bit at first began to bug me more. I began to see differences between what people said and what they did, and some of us lied and some of us stole and a lot of us weren't nice to one another. Some of the leaders were still adulterers or even became adulterers with each other.

But also there were new things they were teaching. The Bible, which had been dictated by God, was infallible and to be taken literally, every word. However, the prophetic books (Daniel, Ezekiel, Revelation, etc.), because they had been written long ago but were actually about things that were going to happen in the future, i.e. now, were written in symbols that had to be interpreted. God had given the gift of interpreting prophesy to a man named Hal Lindsay who wrote a book called *The Late Great Planet Earth* that told us what God had meant when he wrote about the Whore of Babylon, the Mark of the Beast, the Four Horsemen, the Seven Trumpets, etc.[5] These things were about the End Times which were coming soon. The Bible had foretold the founding of the state of Israel in 1948, the E.E.C. and communism and other things happening in our world right now that were preparing the way for the Second Coming, the Rapture, the

AntiChrist, Armageddon, the Tribulation, and the end of the world as we know it.

At the same time we were being taught this stuff in God Squad, in school I was reading poetry by Carl Sandburg and Edna St. Vincent Millay, and novels like *Ethan Frome* and *The Lord of the Flies*. Our English teacher, who called us "you people" as if we were adults, was teaching us about metaphors and symbols and how words could mean something bigger than just what they said literally and that in a good book you didn't read just the words, you also read the ideas behind the words. Sometimes, too, writers left things ambiguous so you would think about them.

As God Squad seemed to talk less about what Jesus did and more about what He was going to do when He came back, and as the Jesus movement waned, I began listening to new things my brother and sister and mother, who had gone back to college herself, were learning about people like Hermann Hesse and Jimi Hendrix and ideas like questioning authority and the military industrial complex and over-throwing the patriarchy.

By the time I went to college I was no longer a fundamentalist, which was good because that was about the worst thing in the world to the feminists and gays and bi's and artists I was starting to hang around with. I was embarrassed about my Christian past and didn't talk about it with anyone.

But part of me also missed it.

I missed having faith in something and believing things could turn out right over time.

About ten years later, in the mid-1980s, after some bad years for me personally, I moved to Europe and got to start my life over again. I lived alone in London for two and a half years. For the first several months I was there, when I was coming out of that bad time, I had a kind of numbing, cottony coating all over me that separated me from things. It covered me up when I needed it to and kept me away from things on days I couldn't get out of bed.

I had two good friends in London whom I had known since I was a kid, and I would see them sometimes, but most of my time I spent alone. I lived alone, I worked alone, I spent a lot of time walking around being a tourist alone. I looked at a lot of art and a lot of buildings.

I started going into the buildings, many of which were churches. At first I went in to look at the architecture. I think I went to every Christopher Wren church in the city. After a while, I went in to hear the music. Most nights of the week, there was some kind of concert or evensong. I started getting up early on Sundays to go hear the big choral masses. And then I wasn't only listening to the music, I was also listening to the words. Then—and this is the only way to describe it—I fell in love with the words. I fell in love with them. I said them over and over in my head the way you would say the name of your beloved. I loved the sounds again of words like "succor" and "beseech" and "comfort ye." I began to look forward all day to going to choral evensong. I loved the opening line, "Oh Lord open thou our lips and our mouths shall show forth thy praise," so much that I almost couldn't stand hearing it. I loved the idea of Someone—God?—opening our mouths, my mouth, and making me speak. Of Him knowing what I wanted and needed to say before I did. I loved the phrase: "Light in our darkness, we beseech thee oh Lord." I loved how it sounded like a pun, and how it addressed God as Light: You are the light in our darkness. But also how it sounded like "Lighten our darkness, please," a begging, an imperative, "God, help me not be in such darkness, please. En-lighten me." I said those words inside my head again and again and again. I looked forward to repeating them out loud with other humans.

I remember one time sitting in a cathedral during service and looking up at the stained-glass window to my right and seeing a pure, clear stream of colored light come through the window as we were saying the words, "Lighten our darkness," and I believed it was happening.

God was Word. He was the impulse to listen to the world and be aware of mystery and grandeur. Jesus was this word made flesh, a human being whose life was about compassion and forgiveness. Christianity was a narrative of conflict, climax and resolution, a story I could understand and love.

A few years ago, after I came back from Europe and began to listen to Mendelssohn and read Lao Tzu and think about what they were saying about words and silence, I got confused.[6] I worried that words, a way by which I had always learned, but which, since my days as a fundamentalist I was afraid to read too literally, could lead me not only not toward, but actually away from God. I worried I had, again, fallen too much in love with certain words and would forget what was before or underneath them.

But Mendelssohn had to use words to tell a friend about his *Songs without Words* and Lao Tzu used words to warn us against relying too much on them. Now I think that words can be a way to point toward God, and a story, like the Christian one, can tell, in a way I understand, about encountering a God who always was and is and does not need our telling.

NOTES

1 The Mendelssohn letter is as quoted in *Felix Mendelssohn and His Times* by Heinrich Edward Jacob, translated by Richard and Clara Winston (Prentice-Hall, 1963), pp. 185–186.

2 *Songs without Words* as performed by Daniel Barenboim (Deutsche Gramophone, #423 931-2, recorded in 1974).

3 There are a million translations of the Tao Te Ching. I am quoting from page 25 of *Tao Te Ching: The Classic Book of Integrity and The Way: Lao Tzu*, translated by Victor H. Mair (Bantam, 1990).

4 Americans have been "witnessing" to each other since before we were even Americans. In the seventeenth century, if you wanted to join some of those colonial Puritan churches, you had to stand up in front of the congregation and tell about your sinful past and then how God had rescued you. The Colonial Captivity Narrative (I-was-kidnapped-by-Indian-Savages-then-rescued-and-returned-to-civilization) and nineteenth-century slave narratives also derive from this particularly American impulse to tell your personal story of hardship, degradation and triumph. There is a direct line between these pre-twentieth-century story forms and the Coming Out Story, the Abuse Survival Story, and the Twelve-step Drunk-a-logue.

But, because Americans always like things Bigger! Louder! More!, our confessions of darkness and redemption have morphed from being confessions to a chosen congregation, into appalling performances overshared with anyone who tunes into Jerry Springer, Dr. Phil, Judge Judy, et al.

Do we do dirt now in order to tell it? (Confession as titillation, exhibition.)

What happens when we're merely saved, but not from any lion's den? Or when your sins are not as gruesome as another's? Are you less saved than they are? What happens if you're happy or content? What happens if you choose to not confess?

(One who knows does not speak; one who speaks does not know.)

Protestantism is a rejection by the individual of the authority of history. The *individual* nature of salvation was especially important to the losers and fanatics, the disgruntled and the second sons who flocked to the "New World" in order to, with their own bare hands, create a rich life of their own. How much more fair this would be than the Old World, in which your future was determined by what your father had been and what he had or hadn't passed on to you. (They used to quip in God Squad, "There's no salvation on the family plan!") If the Old World was about respecting the culture of your elders, the New World was about making your own way as a rugged individual, and if you couldn't make it on your own, then to hell with you.

For more on Puritan life stories/spiritual autobiographies, read Perry Miller. In his introduction to a selection in *The American Puritans: Their Prose and Poetry* (Anchor Books, 1956), Miller talks about how the life stories Puritans told were meant to be "*exemplum*—whether for good or evil; [they] had to be organized into a drama" (p. 225). Who knew the Puritans were such drama queens! Another thing that hasn't changed, or maybe only changed in formal terms: "Almost every Puritan kept a diary, not so much because he was infatuated with himself but because he needed a strict account of God's dealings with him" (pp. 225–226), the modern equivalent being that almost everyone in America is writing a memoir. We, however, do so precisely because we are infatuated with ourselves.

For misbehaving Puritans, read Kai T. Erikson's *Wayward Puritans: A Study in the Sociology of Deviance* (John Wiley & Sons, 1966).

For the history of later conversion narratives in the United States, read Virginia Lieson Brereton's *From Sin to Salvation: Stories of Women's Conversions, 1800 to the Present* (Indiana University Press, 1991). She quotes Jonathan Edwards: "There is no one thing that I know of which God had made such a means of promoting his work among us, as the news of others conversions" (p. 3). Brereton goes on to talk about how the conversion story was often a "public exercise" that "had to be accessible" (pp. 4–5). As if they were just waiting for TV.

5 As it was explained to us, and is still explained to millions of people all over the world, if you are not a Christian when you die, you are going straight to hell. If you are not a Christian when the Rapture happens, you are going to live in a kind of hell on earth for a long and terrible time.

Though the phrase "the Rapture" does not appear in the Bible, ever since the nineteenth-century Dispensationalist movement evangelical Christians have been talking about the time when God would swoop Christians up into the air and His heavenly Kingdom while leaving behind the unsaved to suffer the tribulation of the End Times. Hal Lindsay's *The Late Great Planet Earth* explained how this was going to happen. Originally published in 1970 by Zondervan, a tiny religious press, the book was picked up by Bantam in 1973 and then it really took off. By the 1990s it had sold nearly thirty million copies worldwide. Hal Lindsay, a former tugboat captain and University of Houston dropout, was cited as the author, but over the decades there were mumblings that he had not actually written it. Current reprints of *The Late Great Planet Earth* now credit Lindsay with a "co-author," C. C. Carlson. This same Carlson, it turns out, has ghosted or cowritten or written a number of other books. Back in the '70s, however, there was some issue about not wanting it to be known that the foremost interpreter of fundamentalist Bible prophecy was—that first C. stands for "Carole"—a member of the same gender that was supposed to be subservient to her husband and not speak up in church.

6 Most of what Mendelssohn wrote was without words. Though he set a bunch of songs to words, wrote a couple of oratorios and even included words in his second "Hymn of Praise" symphony, he never wrote a complete opera, which may be why my father was never a fan. My father was a fan of opera—the Italians and Mozart. He didn't care about the stories or the words. For him it was all about singing,

especially the ensembles when three, then four singers, then maybe even five or six, would stack up, playing with and around and against each other in that amazing kind of manic, controlled chaos. My father would listen and chortle "My God, that's beautiful!" and he'd be truly happy.

When I learned this about my father—we'd been on the outs for a while—I was thrilled. I didn't remember him listening to opera when we were growing up, only horrible dentists' office "soft jazz," Swingle Singers and Martin Denny-type stuff on our Family Entertainment Console. He hated our music (Beatles, Hendrix, Rolling Stones) as much as we hated his.

But then he left and then I left and when we got back in touch years later we'd both started listening to opera. He'd listened at home to his records while his wife read on the couch; I'd gone with friends to see it live in day-of-show cheap seats. My father studied the singers and conductors and knew the great performances. I'd thought and talked with my friends about the Great Themes, like the English Lit grads we were. "Yeah, yeah. . ." my father would mumble if I started in on one of my pompous analyses, "Now, listen to this!" and then he'd play some vocal—regardless of the words—that sounded like it was being beamed to us from heaven.

It took me a long time after I left home to forgive my father's leaving. I blamed him for years for something, though now I can't remember exactly what. I had fantasies that one day he and I would have some great, in-depth conversation in which I told—what?—all of how I felt, and he listened attentively and apologized for—what? For being the kind of man he was, living in the time he was and trapped in a family to which he did not belong? It took me less time to get over God and to forgive Him (Father? Son?) for the things I had attributed to Him.

These changes happened over time; they were not brought about through words.

The old books would have been worth nothing at an auction . . .

I burrowed among these venerable books in search of any living thought which should burn like coal or fire or glow like an inextinguishable gem beneath the dead trumpery that had long hidden it. But I found no such treasure; all was dead alike; and I could not but muse deeply and wondering upon the humiliating fact that the works of man's intellect decay like those of his hands. . . . [s]uch books. . . . have, therefore, so little business to be written at all. . . . yet there lingers with me a superstitious reverence for literature of all kinds.

—Nathaniel Hawthorne, "The Old Manse"

Extreme Reading

You eat because you have to, it sustains you. But once you get past the basics of hydration and calories, what you eat and how you eat are determined by your own peculiar, and in the most literal sense, taste, by what can satisfy your sweet tooth or your sour tooth, your savory or unsavory desires. You eat some things because they're good for you, but there are only so many hours in a day, so many days in a life, so you also consume other things solely because you want to, because you have some craving or urge or longing that only this particular thing can fulfill. To be polite you'll eat whatever the people who invited you to dinner at their house have made for you, but when you go out you won't order something you don't like, and if something shows up on your plate in some brownish sauce or gelatinous pool or that gets in your craw or goes down wrong or doesn't appeal, you turn away from it, discreetly if you can, but if you can't, if push comes to shove, if spit comes to fore, you hawk it or gag it or cough it out and you don't care who's watching.

I can't finish books I think are bad. I can't get through somebody's prose that reads to me like Sucaryl or some brownish lumpy sauce or is salt-and-peppered or soy-sauced beyond a shadow of its former self, that's watered down or stupid or pretentious.

Anthropologically speaking, we all recognize there are taboos regarding what we should not eat.

But no one agrees about everything.

We're taught to read because we need to to navigate our culture, to read road signs and the names of stuff at the grocery store, to sign our names on documents when we marry or when we ought to be able to marry. This kind of reading is like hydration and calories. You need it to survive. If you don't get it you get rickets. If you are illiterate you are probably poor, you're missing something basic from your diet and you'll probably die sooner than you should.

But then after we've taken care of our basic needs, we're taught to read in ways that are "good for us," to provide us with a grounding in the humanities, to broaden our minds, etc., then finally to give us pleasure. At this level we decide what we like: chicken or fish, poached or grilled, comics or Rilke, the *New York Times*, the Bible, Barbara Cartland, tacos, cheese.

Extreme reading is like cannibalism. You take a book, like a piece of food, and eat it. For sustenance, for blood, if not to ritually ingest the soul or heart or power of your enemy or someone you loved. You take it in and chew and grind and tear it down to the smallish bits, to things that you can swallow. Your rid yourself of some of it and keep some of the rest. Sometimes you keep what may not be the best for you. Your body knows what's good for you, but sometimes you don't listen. The things you eat and keep become a part of you. You re-create inside yourself, with caverns, juices, processes you can and can't control, a kind of meat.

A book is a thing that someone made from words you think you understand. You take it in and think you are sophisticated, a connoisseur, or at least someone with manners enough to wield a knife and fork and not talk with your mouth full. You know that whatever it is, a ham and cheese on rye, or popcorn or *foie de* something, no matter how humble or fine, you'll break it into broken things that can be used by you and your voracious flesh.

When you read a book, you read what someone else wrote, but you also read your own book. You may read all the words or not, but the words you keep—those that stick to your ribs and keep you awake, dyspeptic, bilious, or that nourish you as if to health, become your muscle, bone or heart—are words you shape as you desire. The book you read is what you want; you will it to your own.

Every time you read a book you read what you desire.
Every time you read a book you make that book your own.

One weekend when I was a teenager, I was sitting alone on a bus on my way to my first Bible Camp Youth Retreat. Most of the other kids on the bus—Texas natives or come-heres from somewhere else in the Bible Belt—had been raised in Christian households, but a few of us were recent converts. Though I believed a lot of what Christians were supposed to, I had trouble with the heaven and hell thing. This may have been part of the reason I was sitting apart from the kids singing Christian songs or doing Bible study, but I was also alone because I was reading a book that was not the Bible, but something my sister had just finished reading in college, *A Portrait of the Artist as a Young Man*.[1] As our bus hurtled through the steamy, spice-scented night toward the East Texas piney woods, I read about Stephen Dedalus and his family and Ireland and food and I came to this:

> Now what is the meaning of this word retreat and why is it . . . a practice of all who desire to lead before God and in the eyes of men a truly Christian life? A retreat, my dear boys, signifies a withdrawal for a while from the cares of our life, the cares of this workaday world, in order to examine the state of our conscience, to reflect on the mysteries of holy religion and to understand better why we are here in this world. During these few days I intend to put before you some thoughts concerning the four last things . . . death, judgment, hell and heaven.

Was it a coincidence that I was reading these words about Stephen Dedalus going on a Christian retreat to learn about heaven and hell at exactly the moment as I myself was going on a Christian retreat and worried about heaven and hell? Or had God arranged for me to read these words right here and now because He was trying to tell me something?

A little later I read this:

> Now let us try for a moment to realize, as far as we can, the nature of that abode of the damned which the justice of an offended God has called into existence for the eternal punishment of sinners. Hell is a strait and dark and foul-smelling prison, an abode of demons and lost souls, filled

with fire and smoke. The straitness of this prisonhouse is expressly designed by God to punish those who refused to be bound by His laws.

I knew that God sometimes spoke to His children in signs. Was God using these words in this book to say something to me? Or was I only hoping or fearing that He was? I don't remember much else about that weekend besides reading those passages over and over and over to myself.

I do not remember what I decided.

When I reread *A Portrait of the Artist as a Young Man* several years later, I could hardly believe it was the same book. The words on the page hadn't changed of course, but I had. Having abandoned my Christian faith, I read a romantic, very male tale of the self and home and family, of nostalgia, growing up and art and God and loss.

Every book you read contains the story of your life.
Every book you read you make your own.

I left home, read a lot and lost my faith. I became a writer and hung around with artists. One time, I went with a bunch of artist pals to the town dump. My visual artist friends had to pay the dump for the things they scavenged—bedsprings and auto parts, engines and tool handles and fence posts—whereas the dump was giving away the books. They were trying to get rid of them. Unlike the materials the artists wanted, the books did not have neat little hinges or squeaky things, they only had wilted, moldy, dirty or stuck-together pages. You couldn't make something cool out of books that you could stand up in your yard or hang your coat on or put flowers in. The books were taking up room and creating a fire hazard. No one had read them for years and probably no one was ever going to read them again. These books were utterly useless. I loved them for that. I think I also felt kind of sorry for them. I took some home.

I felt sorry for some and had contempt for others. For some books I felt both. I thought about how there are so many books out there and how my work would never measure up. But also how there were so many books that were just plain shitty, worse than anything I or anyone I knew would write on our very worst day, yet those shitty books got published and people even bought them, while some actually great books languished in libraries, unchecked-out for years, then got tossed into some twenty-five-cent sale bin or thrown out to the dump. Was this what I wanted my life to be about?

I got a bunch of these books and pens and glue and crayons and tape and invited friends over to my apartment to mess these books up. Some of us "illuminated" our own books, and some we made together. We gave them to each other or slipped them onto the shelves of used bookstores or libraries and fantasized what would happen when someone found them. These cut-and-paste books or illuminated manuscripts or what a librarian friend of mine calls defaced books and artists call "altered texts" or "erasures" are all variations of the kinds of things Orton and Halliwell[2] did and the great Tom Phillips[3] is doing. The story about Orton and Halliwell is that their defacing was prompted by trying to check out some actual literature at the Islington library and being informed that their branch didn't stock whatever they were looking for although it did have all kinds of stupid tripe. Which the couple checked out, doctored and returned. Some of the extreme reading/book demolition my friends and I enjoyed had elements of lit crit or political commentary, like bringing forward the gay subtext in the novel of a closeted writer we knew or splicing a photography book about World War II with one about Japanese flower arranging, but mostly we were just having fun while we drank.

One of those old books from the dump came to my rescue.

For a long time after my parents died I wasn't good for much. Some days I didn't get out of bed. I lost my keys a lot. I watched a lot of videos and took a lot of walks. I'd walk downtown or to the water and sometimes drive out of the city. One time I was at some pretty place— a mountain view or by the sea—and there was one of those benches people put up with a plaque on it that says, "In memory of so 'n' so, who used to love this place." I'd seen those benches and read those words a million times, but this time, when I read the words, I lost it. It had never registered with me before that every one of those nice memorial benches was for someone who was dead, someone whose dying had left behind other people who were knocked out by that death. The words, the bench, the pretty place where once I would have thought, "Oh, what a nice place to sit," were all the same, but after my parents were dead, I wasn't. I just keeled over and bawled my weepy eyes out.

For a long time after my parents died, I also couldn't read. I could flip through magazines or stare at the backs of cereal boxes and even read liner notes, but books were too much. They took concentration and an ability to track and to remember, and if they had stories, the stories were wrong. Or perhaps I should say what the words added up to was wrong, although not every single word was wrong, because some words were right. As I tried to read, the wrong words faded or disappeared, leaving only the horrible right ones.

I picked up one of those old twenty-five-cent books I had lying around and, though I couldn't really read it, individual words jumped out at me. Words like "dead" or "mother" or "no." Or "gone" or "father" or "dead." I started going through the book and finding the words in it that made sense to me. I discovered that the book was, unbeknownst to itself, telling exactly the story of what I was feeling and not feeling and remembering. There were other words between, within the words that were telling something useful to me. It started in the title, *The Mortal Storm*,[4] a novel about heroic people fighting proto-Nazis in the '30s. But actually of course, *The Mortal Storm* contained a book for me, *The MortalS*, less a narrative than a collection of fragments about the deaths of my parents.

Here are my severe edits of the 1,000 or so words that make up the first three pages:

a long   illness
She lay quite still
What happened to   her
mother
would lie   remembering in   the bed
mother   sick
it's all over now   mother
Nothing can be helped
    dead   dying   dead   dead
her mother   her mother   her mother

And so on.

It took me a few years to cut and paste (the term I prefer to "erasure" or "altered text" because it sounds more like what you did in grade school and less like something that you are going to call Art), through the entirety of *The MortalS*, during which I got past much of my parents' deaths. I believe that being able to, however thoughtlessly or subconsciously, engage with others' words and find the words

I needed in them helped me obsess over or meditate my way through my sadness.

A few years later, though I had stopped having cut-and-paste parties, I still kept at it on my own. The next book I completed I'd bought for a dollar at a used bookstore in Vermont. *I Want to Be a Lady* by Maximilian Foster (J. B. Lippincott Company, 1926), is a comic western romance that tells the story of an Eastern girl who, in late nineteenth-century America, goes west where she encounters a group of lovable cowboys and scrappy, "unladylike" frontier folk. Though our heroine wants to be a lady (i.e., live a genteel, back-east-style life), she realizes that the lovable cowboys and scrappy frontier folk are warm-hearted and good and she is happier being the honest frontier wife of a lovable cowboy than a proper back-east Lady. *I Want to Be a Lady*, however, contains within it an entirely other book, which I discovered through severe editing. I went through the book, page by page, for more than a year, and painted or colored or collaged over most of the words, leaving only the words that told the story I needed to tell. My book, the book I desired, contained therein, is titled, *I Want a Lady* and it is a woeful autobiography about a doomed lesbian romance I had with an older—uh—lady, when I was young and still believed the words that books and people said.

Every time you read a book you read what you desire.
Every book you read includes the story of your life.

NOTES

1 The *A Portrait of the Artist as a Young Man* I read these days is not my sister's copy, though I thank her for the loan and for a million others. (Lawrence Ferlinghetti's *A Coney Island of the Mind*, Aldous Huxley, Margaret Atwood, etc.; tons of music—the Beatles and the Rolling Stones, then Hendrix, Simon and Garfunkel, Jethro Tull.) My reading copy is, rather, included in *The Portable James Joyce* (Viking, 1966), edited and with an introduction and notes by Harry Levin, the same guy who did my Hawthorne Riverside anthology (that guy gets around!) which I purchased, used, for the pathetic sum of $6.60.

2 The altered texts made by playwright Joe Orton and his lover Kenneth Halliwell are described in John Lahr's terrific biography *Prick Up Your Ears* (Knopf, 1978). Orton and Halliwell, before the one whacked the other to death with a hammer, lived in a tiny little flat in Islington, the same part of London where I lived in the '80s. I went to what had been their place and stood outside and looked at it. I went to the library too. Though the artful altering of shitty library books earned Orton time in the slammer, those same defaced books, once evidence of criminal destruction of property, are now the crown jewels of the Islington library.

3 Tom Phillips's great and beautiful altered text, the daddy of them all, is *A Humument*, which you should look up at www.tomphillips. co.uk and humument.com.

4 *The Mortal Storm* (Little, Brown, 1938) is probably the most well-known of the many, many books by Phyllis Bottome, the British daughter of an American clergyman. Bottome's output included novels, short fiction and a biography of the man with whom she studied psychoanalysis in Vienna, Alfred Adler. In 1940, the unabashedly anti-Nazi *Mortal Storm* was made into a film starring James Stewart as a good German who doesn't join the Nazis, and Margaret Sullivan as the non-German (read Jewish) girl with whom he falls in love. The movie pissed the Nazis off so much that they banned all MGM films from being shown in Germany. *The Mortal Storm* isn't banned anywhere anymore but it might as well be, in the sense that we can't find it readily because our tastes have changed and now it comes across as just a toothless bit of cinematic junk food.

Our ghost . . . was invisible.
　　　—*Nathaniel Hawthorne, "The Old Manse"*

Invisible

"Oh darn, I'm still invisible!"
—The Invisible Woman, Universal Pictures, 1940[1]

They looked through her like she wasn't there.
As if the Invisible Woman did not exist.

Actually, it wasn't neutral like that. It was like she was a worm. Unsightly. Less than dirt. Grotesque.[2]

Actually they did see her, but only for an instant, the flick of a movie frame that nobody sees, though of course everyone does see in some subliminal way, but only registers when something is wrong with the projector or when there's something bad in the air, a pollutant, something poisonous, after the discovery of which everyone looks away either irritated, pissed off, offended and demanding their money back, or, if they are kind, or sympathetic as a saint, either pretending not to have seen or if having seen then also to have seen past the problem, whether the brief, fixable one as in the case of the projector and/or atmosphere or the long- (if not forever) term, inherent, unfix-able one as in the case of the Invisible Woman.

This looking is done—I'm talking about away from the Invisible Woman now, not the movie projector—so as not to embarrass or make uncomfortable anyone. For what is "seen," i.e., the Invisible Woman, is so perverse, unnerving, grotesque and so on, that it renders everyone, that is, some people, speechless.

Then there is their seeing but wishing they hadn't, and then their pretending they hadn't, then looking away—the whip of the head, the spin of the hips—which makes their not entirely graceful selves bumble and stumble around like a bunch of bumpkins. Look how they fall all over themselves! All over one another! It's kind of funny, really, the way they flail around as if the floor is covered with banana peels. They look like the Keystone Cops! Like Charlie Chaplin in that fac-tory scene, or is it the meal scene, when everything—soup, glasses, plates, spoons—keeps flying at him from the conveyer belt. Like the cat's eyeballs when the kid takes it out of the dryer. They fall all over themselves as they scramble to get out of the factory, the kitchen, the courtroom, the theater, studio, tavern, bar, bedroom, her bedroom, bed, her bed, The Invisible Woman's bed.

How on earth did they get there?

None of us is stupid anymore. We know what brought them here and know as well how desperate they all are to get away. For what if someone saw them here? With the Invisible Woman? How would they explain? That they have "a scientific interest"? Or "are interested in learning about all of humankind, even in its most egregious, filthy forms?" Or are just "curious"?

As if we don't all know what killed the cat.

For One—not her real name—is curious. Not only that, is so inclined. And goes, therefore, in secret, ashamed, to meet the Invisible Woman.

One meets her in the dark of night, in a bar across the tracks. One meets her where the poor folks live, the dive down by the docks. Self-loathingly, her-loathingly, One goes to get the thing One needs from her.

One hates to want the way one does
thus being one whom One revileth.
No wonder One will not admit her kind.

One—not her real name—has good reasons, One tells oneself: it's nobody's business, it's private and no one else would really understand. Besides, One tells oneself, I'm not like them.

One never will admit, at least not until One has to because it's about to be splashed all over the department, the neighborhood, the soon-to-be published unauthorized biography[3] or mistakenly (har har) over the intercom,[4] or in the courtroom, the rehab farm, ("It wasn't really me, it was the alcohol … and … my … um … tragic childhood")[5], etc., ad nauseam. Then One will scramble again, the way One did when one was first seen in the Invisible Woman's company, and treat us, again, to yet another almost laughable, were it not so damned offensive, festival of lies.

As if anyone with half a brain would believe One.

For everyone with half a brain had figured One out long ago and was like, Do you think you're kidding anyone any more? Get over yourself, you spineless shit.

No wonder she's invisible.

Though, admittedly, even we didn't see her at first.

Or saw her only from the corners of our eyes, while looking furtively. For we'd been told to look away and did until we couldn't anymore for we were pulled. Then glimpsed in fear then longer looks then weirded out then panicked then with recognition, awe, and then at last with eagerness, overt and sloppy, slobbering like a puppy on a leash.

Then once we knew the way we were and ways we were not them, we thought of bigger things. Then either decided or realized there were ways we did not want to be either like or part of them. We had our reasons. We talked about these reasons very loudly, very earnestly, sometimes over the top-ly, and frankly, retrospectively, overbearingly. We may have done silly or even arrogant, as is the way of youth, things, but whatever, we did not—ever—lie.

For lying there is no excuse.

Well, maybe a few.

Such as youth. But then everyone grows up, right? Even One. Or such as when in some places you need to in order to not be shot, have your hands cut off or something rammed up you (in order to show you what it's like to be a real something or to, uh, encourage you to not) or tied to a fence, beaten and left to bleed and/or freeze to death. In cases such as these it is not only permissible, it is very strongly advisable to tell those thuggy Cro-Magnon fuckers whatever they want to hear. Lie through your teeth if it'll keep you alive and then as soon as you can, get the hell out of there and never, ever go back. In situations like that "lying" isn't lying, it's life-saving.

However, lying *is* lying if the only thing one may perhaps lose is a bit of cash, a contract, one's "reputation."

Which will then eventually be that of a lying, first-class coward.

For lying like that, for then continuing to lie when everyone else with even half a ball is beginning to tell the truth, there is no excuse. Not one.

For others had begun to tell the truth and therefore other others looked and then began to see, then other others also did, then more and more and then, gosh, Invisible Women were popping up all over the place! Not only down across the tracks or where the sailors went, but also in the studio, the academy, the theater, the library, the bed, the bed, the bed.

One's bed.

This made One nervous. Why wouldn't those unsightly ones just stay quiet about it? Why rub everyone's nose in it? Why not just mind their own business?

Because it *was* their business. As it was One's. For One was one and lots of people knew it. Which made One really, really nervous.

One told oneself that One wasn't like the rest. Which of course was partly true in that One was not like those who told the truth. However One *was* like those who were intelligent, creative, magnetic, etc., which begs the question, what exactly was it about them that One found so grotesque?

For One was not above us, or so different from the way we were. No, One was, rather, among us (slumming?) frequently, in all places we were found—across the tracks, down by the docks, inside our bed.

For One was one of us. Yes. Yes, you were.

You met the Invisible Woman late at night. You went to her to get from her the thing you hated wanting. You did with her the truest thing that made you who you were.

Then every kiss she gave you, you denied.

◆   ◆   ◆

The Invisible Woman arrives in town late on a winter night. There's snow on the ground and the wind is high and everything is black and white and gray. We see the prints her feet leave in the snow as she walks the lonely road up into town. The wind is howling, pushing her, but she has had to learn to push back hard against it. She's covered completely from head to toe—a long wool coat and low-brimmed hat, a scarf around her face. Black glasses, almost goggle-like. A heavy pair of gloves. There's no place where her skin's exposed. She carries a doctor's bag. She opens the door and the wind howls in. In the kitchen, the barman's wife shuts her eyes and sighs in sweet relief. At last! The conversation in the pub goes quiet. The locals are used to strangers here, especially at night, but even so, they all look up to see who's just arrived. Everybody stops and stares, the pints upraised in drinkers' paws, the dart about to fly. Even the snuffling dog looks up but oddly, though his human companions believe this is a stranger, sniffs a single, recognizing sniff, then lowers its head contentedly and shuts his trusting eyes. No one can tell, but no one wonders, whether the stranger is a woman or a man.

The Invisible Woman asks for a room. "Of course, Doctor," the barman says and goes to get the key. But you, the dutiful barman's wife, tell him he's busy, dear, so you'll see to the guest.

Besides, you know, as the clueless yobs that drink here every night do not, this guest has come for you.

You also know the sweet and unsuspecting stepdad of your son won't notice, as he has not before, you grab a bottle of something nice—champagne? a vintage port? a fabulous old claret?—to steal up to the room.

"My bags are at the station," the Invisible Woman says, "Can you bring them up?"

"Not 'til tomorrow, I'm afraid," the barman says, "There won't be anyone there until the next train's due in the morning. Don't worry about them, though, ours is a trusting town."

The Invisible Woman attempts to sound disgruntled.

You gesture for her to follow you; you'll show her to the room.

"What took you so long," you whisper nervously as soon as you're out of earshot.

"The storm," the Invisible Woman says. You fear someday that the Invisible Woman will be caught. Then who will be your paramour? Who else will know and tolerate your lies?

You lead the way up the winding stairs. You know that with your each and every step the Invisible Woman behind you is watching the sassing of your hips, the swish of your skirt and breathing the milky scent of your perfect skin. You lead her to "our" room as you and she, after all this time, refer to it. Amazing how your husband(s, and there've been a few, they somehow never last) has never noticed how often bulkily clad strangers come to town and how oddly gruff yet oddly high and curiously alike their voices are.

Once in the room, you close the door behind you both and lock it. You double the lock and put the key in your apron pocket. You show the Invisible Woman the closet (har), the table, sink, the bed, the bed, the bed. Your bed.

You don't dive into it just yet, but coyly, as if the ingenue, go to the window and gaze out at the stormy sky. Making sure to present your best side, you pose and consider how the romantic, *sturmy und drangy* sky will frame you.

The snow's still falling hard and fast. You say, in your best, though not very good, Bacall, "It's going to be a long, cold night," and though you're still facing away from the Invisible Woman, a smile plays across your face. You're not, of course, saying this for her, but for the camera rolling in your head that's filming the epic movie starring you. How to play it this time? Your charming, elegant, witty self? Or your sultry, world-weary sophisticate? Innocent or jaded? Sweet or cynical? Bold or shy? Crusader for the truth, though that one's rather difficult . . . For you are very versatile. The rest of us know that no one can be all things to all people without being any one at all. But that doesn't stop you from trying. You close the curtains and turn to your Invisible Woman who is still standing in her clothes.

That's weird. Usually by this time she's naked in your bed. Usually by now the most we can see is the shape of her body beneath the sheet and the pillow's slight depression. Tonight, however, she's still in full Invisible regalia: coat, scarf, glasses, gloves, etc., and looking, at least her glasses appear to be, straight at you. You can't tell, because of the glasses, the kind a blind girl wears, if she is looking away from, at or through you.

As if you are not there. Or don't exist.

Suddenly you're uncomfortable and look down at yourself. You are wearing your dress, your apron and gloves (necessary for anyone who works in food preparation), your stockings, shoes, etc. You are still fully covered.

Composure regained, you ask, "What's taking you so long?"

"I was wondering," your guest replies, "if this time you would undress first. In the light."

You haven't. Not for ages.

"No," you tell her. "No." For a moment she doesn't move. "I'll check the door again," you say. You always worry about the lock; the Invisible Woman doesn't.

The Invisible Woman sighs, then slowly, reluctantly, slides off a glove. We see the empty, open, hollow sleeve. The other glove comes off and, after they are both dropped to the floor, we see a pair of empty sleeves. The end of one of the empty sleeves appears to remove her glasses. Where her eyes should be is only dark, two empty sockets framed by gauze. She lifts a hand we can't see to remove the scarf that covers the lower half of her face. Around the hole where no mouth is, an edge of gauze appears to puff, then there's a rising and a fall as if an opening and closing of her mouth, as if a pair of lips. There is the sound of a moving tongue, of air pushed over teeth, of breath, a swallowing.

The Invisible Woman is trying to tell you something.

You won't hear.

"Come *on*," you say impatiently. You're not here in this room to chat.

There is another pause—as if she hopes—but then another tug, a lift of a flap and the gauze around her invisible head unravels and unravels into nothing. And then the hands that we can't see unbutton the headless overcoat and drop it to the floor. The pants kick off the shoes, unzip and drop to the floor. The long-tailed shirt unbuttons itself and falls to the floor and we see no one. Then there is a sound of the mattress being sat upon, the sight of slight depression in the bed, the shape of a head on the pillow.

You open a bottle and pour a couple of drinks. You hand one to your invisible guest but tonight she doesn't take it. When you have had a few, and hers as well, and heard yourself tell her the things you won't tell anyone else, you check again that the door is locked, turn out the light and undress in the dark.

You get into bed and the Invisible Woman does the thing you want, the thing you told her long ago that made you who you were.

She used to hope that someday you'd stop lying. But she no longer does. She feels your most recent plastic fingernails running down her back and makes herself not twist away.

How long has it been since she's felt your skin? She's beginning to not remember.

You fall asleep, as you usually do. The Invisible Woman doesn't.

She watches you sleep, as if she could see, beneath the things you've done to yourself, the person you once might have been—transparent, without guile. The Invisible Woman loved you once.

When you are sunk in sleep, your breathing low, she runs her hands, not touching, but above and very close to what she remembers of your body, beneath the touch-ups and the patches, grafts, the implants and the silicone. She thinks about how much of you is lost and how what is left is lies.

This time, unlike the previous, you don't wake up and leave her: she leaves you.

She steps over the clothes and bandages on the floor, finds the keys in your apron pocket and lets herself out, naked, of your room. She leaves the door unlocked and she imagines, as she leaves, what happens next.

You are awakened by the sound of someone screaming. The too much that you drank last night has made you oversleep. It's morning and you're still in bed, though not your own. The sheet's tossed back and you're not dressed, so the maid who's entered to do her chores (she knocked, but there was no response, and the door had not been locked) has seen something grotesque, a mess of wig and pancake make-up smeared around as if by a four-year-old. A couple of blue-black smudges beneath a skewed pair of movie-star-thick eyelashes. Scar-covered bulbous silicone boobs and bee-sting lips, a Frankenstein fabrication made of vanity and shame.

The terrified maid runs screaming from the room and, brought by her shouts, your husband appears with a few old sots who've come by for their breakfast.

The Invisible Woman, who loved you once, sees all this from the comfy chair she sits in at the toasty warm cafe at the train station. She waits for the train that will take her far away. She sees, as if by magic, close-up, both in black-and-white and color, the gasps on the faces of those that find you—their mouths open wide in horror, their hands held in front of their eyes as if to push away the sight.

You yank the sheet to cover the bits of you: "It isn't what you think!" you screech, "I can explain!"

But this time, finally, you can't. They see the proof before them of your lies.

We cannot see, not even us, the reaction on the Invisible Woman's face.

But we can guess.

It used to be she pitied you. Not anymore.

NOTES

1 *The Invisible Woman* (1940), Universal Pictures, directed by A. Edward Sutherland, starring Virginia Bruce and John Barrymore, story by Joe May and Kurt Siodmak based on characters created by H. G. Wells)[6] was the second movie to follow James Whale's *The Invisible Man*[7] of 1933. During the 1940s, there were four sequels to Whale's original (all of which you can see together on the Criterion Collection disc), three serious and tragic, or at least intended to be seen as so, and one fluffy romantic comedy, the only one about a woman.

In 1933, Claude Raines played what the opening credits called "The Invisible One." (As if one could be or become something no one else could see and therefore could not tell whether one is man or woman or other.)

It was Raines's first major film role and we don't see him—only hear his voice—until the end of the movie when the Invisible One is killed. It's only then, when dead, that one becomes visible again.

James Whale made movies about monsters—Frankenstein's, Invisible Ones and Men in Iron Masks—who looked not right or just plain wrong or wanted to find a mate like them or not be seen or seen as they were not or born not in the right skin and then were killed.

James Whale was a homosexual.

He was also, like H. G. Wells and Claude Raines, a kid from one class trying to pass for another. To seem to be somebody he was not.

2 When it was first published in 1897, Wells's *The Invisible Man* was subtitled "*A Grotesque Romance*," as if he saw that though we might advance in science, i.e., in how we see ourselves in relation to the universe, matter and time, we would advance less quickly in the ways we see and let ourselves be seen Romantically.

Grotesque is how too many see too many too invisible.

H. G. Wells bios are all over the place, from those little paragraphs in the start of the cheap editions to massive fat hardbacks you can find used. One of the most funs ones is in *Graphic Classics: H. G.*

Wells, Volume Three: The Time Machine, The Invisible Man & Six More Exciting Stories!, 2nd ed., Eureka Productions, 2005. htpp://www.graphicclassics.com. What I especially like about this collection is the fact that they have a cartoony rather than a reproduced photothing of Wells on what in an old-timey book would have been called the frontispiece. There's something about Wells that is suited to this oddly two dimensional face, more like Dr. Spock or Data than some kind of end-of-the-nineteenth-century guy.

Arthur C. Clarke wrote a nice little intro to the Modern Library edition (2000) of *The Invisible Man*, and some unnamed, invisible as it were, poor sod wrote the nice little biographical note.

I wonder what H. G. Wells would have thought of how we read him, what we make of him now a hundred or so years after he invented us, I mean his books invented us. Or saw us. Or saw how we wouldn't see ourselves, each other.

Will what is in the heart remain invisible forever?

3 Susan Sontag, for almost her entire life, had always, when asked about her personal life, foregrounded her one-time marriage to a man and the resulting son. Not until the impending publication of a book-length biography that was going to reveal the many long-term, creatively and intellectually significant relationships Sontag had had with lesbian lovers throughout her life did she, in a pre-book article in the *New Yorker*, publicly admit that she was homo. At which point she fell all over herself to explain that she had never actually *lied* about being in the closet as her gayness had always been a kind of "open secret." She wanted us to know that she had simply chosen not to foreground something "private" (as opposed to a heterosexual marriage, which is not "private"). The latter lie, that she had never been in the closet, the lie we might refer to as the cover-up, is more offensive than the initial lie, i.e., her presumed heterosexuality. Why didn't she, when she finally did come out after all those years, say something such as "I stayed in the closet for decades because if I'd come out earlier, I would have been ghettoized as lesbian and not able to do the work I wanted to do. That I can come out now without losing the respect I have earned as

a thinker is partly due to the work other lesbian and gay people have been doing for decades."

It wasn't like Sontag hadn't known she was gay. The September 10, 2006 issue of the *New York Times Magazine* published excerpts from her diaries that included the following:

Nov. 19: 1959:
"The only kind of writer I could be is the kind who exposes himself."
(Ed. Note: . . . unless that "self" is lesbian.)

Dec. 24, 1959:
"My desire to write is connected with my homosexuality. I need the identity as a weapon, to match the weapon that society has against me."
"I am just becoming aware of how guilty I feel being queer."

Sontag wrote these things a decade before Stonewall and ages before the modern American feminist and gay movements. The point is not that she did not come out in 1959, but that she continued to deny her lesbianism for decades while writing about an "erotics of art," the "revolutionary implications of sexuality in contemporary society," etc. How long was she planning to keep up her charade?

I have felt sorry for self-loathing and/or cowardly homophobes when they have no examples, resources, contexts in which to come out. But when they continue, after having been given lots of examples, resources, contexts, etc., to lie and to ignore the existence of others who were working to make the world better for them, I do not feel sorry for them. I feel, rather, like Get over yourself, you spineless shit.

4 Ellen, a TV character. As in, would Ellen (Rosie, Sontag, whoever) have the career she has now if she had come out at the start of her career? Or would she have been pegged as a homo and not allowed to have a mainstream career at all? Don't get me wrong. I love how Rosie was America's girl next door and then came out as gay, and I love how

Ellen is America's new girl next door. It's true, and it always has been: Jo, who dressed like a boy as much as she could and referred to herself as "the man in the family" in *Little Women*, Nancy Drew's friend George, the Kate Jackson character on *Charlie's Angels*, every single female camp counselor ever. America's girl next door really is a big old chummy dyke.

If only people saw what they were seeing.

Plus, when my mother was dying, she loved watching Rosie because Rosie made her laugh and I was able to sit with my mother and hear her laugh. Plus, when I told my mom that Rosie was gay, as all gays knew before Rosie came out publicly, my mom said, "Really? Well, she seems nice . . ." (Remember when Rosie was "Queen of Nice"? Talk about passing!)

But "niceness" has a ring of willful forgetfulness when someone says, "Gee, I finally, after X years in the closet, came out and everyone has been so nice and accepting of me!" Whereas the reason that person did not come out X years ago was that she would never have been hired or would have been fired or wouldn't have the career she has now or not have access to the people who are so nice to her now.

Quick, name your favorite lesbian TV, movie or mainstream theater actresses who have been out their whole careers! Need a little more time? That's okay. No one else can come up with anyone either.

(BTW: Anyone remember when kd lang was on Rosie? That was funny—watching Rosie scramble to not be near an out lesbian. And how about all those years Rosie was talking about "Ooooh, Tom Cruise!" Actually, that really is pretty funny. They would have been a perfect pair.

But I really, truly do admire her, really and truly. I recognize that she had to do what she did in order to become America's best gay friend.)

Maybe this kind of forgetting is not that different from girls today saying "I'm not a feminist, I just want to be a lawyer," unaware that a generation ago not many girls were able to go to law school.

Is this progress, when things change so much you forget they were ever different?

Is progress everyone else forgetting or never even knowing what you once thought was so important?

Or is it just that I'm getting old?

Maybe this is what getting old means. That one starts wanting other ones, the ones who are replacing one, to know about one's heroic, terrible, glorious past and all the things one did back then to make the world a better place. Or maybe it's wanting to go back, but to a different past, and do things differently. Or maybe it's wishing one had been born later when the things one thought were terrible were over and everything had gotten easier. Or wishing one was someone else because one is a has-been? Or worse, a never-been?

5   Mark Foley, an icky creep, made similar excuses when he was caught bonking interns. Around the same time, there was also that fundamentalist minister, Ted Haggard, who had a long-standing affair with a gay hustler. They took speed together, too, and then, because Haggard was such a vehement opponent of gay marriage, the hustler finally came out with their story. A while after this story broke, I read in the paper that Rev. Haggard, having been through some kind of therapeutic deprogramming, was, and I quote, "completely heterosexual." Praise the Lord!

A few months later, I read that the hustler fellow wrote a book about his relationship with Haggard. I wish him all the best in his literary endeavors.

6   H. G. Wells's *The Invisible Man* was published in 1897, two years after the first of his great science fiction novels, *The Time Machine*. Wells had turned to writing out of desperation. Trained in the sciences and working as a teacher, Wells was stricken with tuberculosis, which meant he had to quit work and spend a lot of time recuperating in bed. Strapped for a way to make a living, he read *When a Man's Single* by J. M Barrie (the same J. M. Barrie of Peter Pan fame, regarding whom we will refrain from making comments as to why such a man might be "single"), which described how to write saleable columns

for newspapers. Wells followed Barrie's advice and was soon selling articles, stories and serials.

Wells's father was, at various times, a gardener, a professional cricket player and a shopkeeper. Wells's mother was a housekeeper and lady's maid. Wells, known as Bert, left school at fourteen to apprentice to a draper, then got a scholarship to the Royal College of Science where he studied with T. H. Huxley, who instilled in Wells a belief in social as well as biological evolution, i.e., the perfectibility of humankind. Nice idea.

On the other hand, "perfectibility," or any form of perfectness, can sound a little scary. As in perfect equals pure, as in the purity of the races, the eradication of imperfect ones, of ones with impure impulses, etc.

One man's purity is another man's filth.

Is history the repeating of the stories we deny?
Do we forget the awful ways we were?

Wells sort of believed in the perfectibility of humankind for a while (*Mankind in the Making*, 1903; *A Modern Utopia*, 1905). He was a socialist and, until he quit after a series of arguments with George Bernard Shaw, a Fabian, a visionary.

The Invisible Man is a book about vision and seeing and not being seen, about who sees whom and when, and what happens when we look away and why. It's about how it isn't just believing but acknowledging what we see, and that we sometimes see things we do not know the names of yet.

In order to belong you must be seen.

The plot: A scientist named Griffin figures out how to become invisible. He makes a potion and does stuff with light and refraction and becomes invisible and it's fun for a while, giving him access to a secret life that no one else can see.

But later on it's not so fun. He can't make himself visible, which cuts him off from things he needs and wants.

In 1895, two years before the publication of *The Invisible Man*, Oscar Wilde was prosecuted for "gross indecency between males." (The big bio of Wilde is Richard Ellmann's *Oscar Wilde* [Vintage, 1988]. There's also some great stuff in *The Wilde Years: Oscar Wilde and His Time*, edited and with text by Tomoko Sato and Lionel Lambourne [Barbican Art Galleries and Philip Wilson Publisher, 2000]. For a general history of homos: *Completely Queer: The Gay and Lesbian Encyclopedia*, Steve Hogan and Lee Hudson [Henry Holt, 1998]). Wilde had fallen in love, in 1891, with a beautiful boy half his age. Lord Alfred "Bosie" Douglas, Wilde wrote, in imagery like that in the play he was writing at the time, was "quite like a narcissus—so white and gold." Wilde began to write his version of the Salome story, in which an old man is destroyed by his desire for a beautiful young thing, shortly after he met Bosie. Bosie was a poet too, and later translated Wilde's *Salome* from its original French into English.

Bosie's father, the Marquis of Queensberry, became convinced that Wilde was corrupting his son, that is, his *other* son. For Bosie was not the only sexually suspicious offspring of the Marquis. The elder brother, Francis Archibald, Viscount Drumlanrig, was reputed to have had an affair, while working as his "private secretary," with the Liberal politician Lord Roseberry. Lord Roseberry became prime minister in 1894 and elevated Francis to Baron Kelhead, thus allowing the son a seat in the House of Lords, an ambition the father had never fulfilled. Queensberry was furious with Francis and his "patron" and threatened to expose the prime minister's taste for young men unless the government prosecuted Wilde. In 1894, Queensberry wrote a letter to Bosie suggesting that "Snob Queers like Roseberry" had turned his sons homo. That same year Francis died in a mysterious hunting accident that may have been suicide.

What had poor old Queensberry, a notorious womanizer and the man who codified the rules of that most macho of sports, boxing, in his magnum opus *Queensberry's Rules*, done so cosmically wrong that both of his boys turned out to be pansies?

Provoked by an insulting telegram from his son Alfred, the Marquis sent a letter to Wilde's club addressed "To Oscar Wilde, posing Somdomite." Not only was the Marquis of Queensberry bad at spelling, he also seemed to think—hope?—that Wilde and Bosie were only pretending to be homos in order to shock people. Which might have made sense because the aesthetician Wilde had suggested that the pose, rather than the fact, was what was important: "To have done it was nothing, but to make people think one had done it was a triumph." In this case, however, Wilde had not been posing, he had been in love.

Queensberry was pushing it to send that card, but Wilde was just plain stupid to do what he did next: he brought a libel suit against Queensberry.

Did Wilde object to the fact that Queensberry suggested he was *only* posing?

Or was Wilde egged on by Bosie because Bosie hated his father and even blamed his father for his older brother's death?

Or did Wilde think that, as a darling of London culture, he could get away with anything?

Or was he really smart, knowing that suing his boyfriend's father would bring it all out in public? "Things are because we see them," Wilde had written in "The Decay of Lying" in 1891, and the trial of 1895 made what had been invisible very seen indeed.

Or was Wilde, in a parallel that could only happen in life because it's just too tidy for fiction, repeating the history of his own father?

In 1864, when Oscar was ten, Wilde senior had his shady sex life put on trial. Sir William Wilde was accused by a girl of seducing her while she was under chloroform. Sir William, like his son when he was brought down later, was at the peak of his career. He was the leading ophthalmologist in Britain, a medical writer and had just been knighted. His wife, now Lady Wilde, was a poet who published under the name "Speranza." She was not, however, the only person writing under that pseudonym. In early 1864 a pamphlet claiming to be the work of "Speranza" accused a "Dr. Quilp" of raping "Miss Price" under chloroform. When Lady Wilde discovered that the pamphleteer was Mary Travers (not the Peter, Paul and Mary one), she wrote a letter to Travers's father denying the pamphlet's "unfounded accusations." (For the Sir William Wilde and Mary Travers material check out Ray J. Defalque and Amos J. Wright, "Travers vs. Wilde: Chloroform Acquitted," *Bulletin of Anesthesia History* 23, no. 4.)

Mary Travers found Lady Wilde's letter and sued her for libel, and Dublin and the British medical world had a trial to salivate over. Though it was widely known that Sir Wilde was a womanizer (he fathered at least three illegitimate kids), and there was evidence that he and Travers had had a long-term—uh—affection of some variety or other, Wilde's wife defended her husband's fidelity. After the five-day trial, the court ruled against Sir Wilde, but, believing Mary may have been a willing participant, the judge made the doctor pay damages of only one farthing (one quarter of a penny). The trial took a toll on Sir Wilde. He lost interest in medicine and twelve years later he died.

Did Father's ghost make Son repeat the cause of family shame? What is it fathers pass on to their kids? What unseen things repeat in them? What history?

Is history the repeating of the stories we deny?
Do we refuse to learn as if we're different?

Or did Oscar Wilde actually want people to think that, as much as he loved beauty, and especially the beauty of boys, he, a married man and father of two, whether posing and/or a "somdomite," could also be an ideal husband?

An Ideal Husband opened in London three months before Wilde had Queensberry arrested for criminal libel. The play was a tremendous success, the trial was swift and the day Queensberry was found innocent Wilde was arrested on the charges of "committing acts of gross indecency with other male persons." Though Wilde's plays continued (*The Importance of Being Earnest* was running in the West End too), his name was removed from the theater marquees.

On the one hand, Wilde was fortunate it was 1895. Until 1861, when the maximum punishment for buggery was reduced to life imprisonment, sodomy had been a capital crime in the UK punishable by hanging. In 1885 the punishment was further reduced to two years hard labor in prison, but the law also expanded the scope of the "crime" from mere buggery to "gross indecency."

During Wilde's first trial for "gross indecency" the jury failed to reach a verdict, and Wilde was tried again. At the second trial he was sentenced to two years hard labor and sent to Reading Gaol. Bosie never visited or wrote to him. Between January and March of 1897, in preparation for his release in May, Wilde wrote, on regulation blue prison paper handed to him one sheet at a time, a long letter to Bosie that was later titled *De Profundis* by Wilde's loyal friend Robert Ross. From that sad book:

> Dear Bosie—After long and fruitless waiting I have determined to write to you myself, as much for your sake as for mine. . . . Our ill fated and most lamentable friendship has ended in ruin and public infamy for me, yet the memory of our ancient affection is often with me, and the thought that loathing, bitterness and contempt should for ever take that place in my heart once held by love is very sad. . . .

By the time he was released from prison in 1897, Wilde's health had gone to hell. He fled to France where, in 1900, wretched and penniless, he died.

The Invisible One is killed becoming visible.

Wilde was not the only literary man who, in 1895, was smithereened by a public who would just as rather he had kept his despicable self invisible. That same year, Thomas Hardy, a mason's son who, despite being from the wrong class, became a writer, published *Jude the Obscure*. This novel is, among other things, a damning look at the strictures of conventional marriage, sex and relationships between the classes. While not vilified as much as Wilde, Hardy was called a "degenerate" in the press and the book itself was renamed (har har) *Jude the Obscene.*

It wasn't that people from different classes had not engaged in romantic or sexual affairs with one another before. What enraged late-nineteenth-century English society was referring to it openly, making it visible.

Wilde's trial made visible around the world the possibility of same-sex love and what might happen to those who might be so inclined. Gertrude Stein was at Radcliffe then, studying the composition, psychology and philosophy that were to have such a tremendous effect on her ideas of perception, repetition and the continuous present. She was also enjoying a lively social life, although, as she later remembered, she became very upset by news of the trial of Oscar Wilde. Was this partly because she sensed that if she ever fell in love, as she would in two short years, the object of her desire would be a person of her own gender?

You mean it is the same.

———————

Yes, I know what your idea is.
Lifting belly knows all about the wind.

———————

Can you suspect me.
We are glad that we do not deceive.

("Lifting Belly," *Gertrude Stein: Writings 1903–1932,* Library of America, 1998)

Around the same time, a strange adolescent named Marguerite was falling in love with an invisible voice. Alberto Visetti, Marguerite's stepfather, had, in 1894, awarded a young woman named Agnes Nicholls a scholarship to the Royal College of Music. While Agnes Nicholls practiced her singing in the Visetti's garden studio, Marguerite listened and, before she even laid eyes on the singer, fell desperately in love.

Years later Marguerite, known to her intimates as John and to her public as Radclyffe Hall, wrote *The Well of Loneliness*, a novel that argued for the sympathetic treatment of "inverts" such as its protagonist, Stephen Gordon, a character who has since been called, depending on who is talking to whom and when and why: lesbian, dyke, queer, woman trapped in the body of a man, passing man, transgendered person, mannish woman and a lot of other things.

Who are you when you are someone who's not been seen before? What are you when the thing you are does not yet have a name?

The Well of Loneliness was published in English in France in July of 1928 and, due to massive sales, went into multiple printings. British publishers had turned it down, but English readers wanted it and copies couldn't arrive from France fast enough. In October, British customs officials seized a shipment of the book at Dover. (For Radclyffe Hall, see Sally Cline, *Radclyffe Hall: A Woman Called John*, Overlook Press, 1998, and the heroic Allison Hennegan's intro to *The Well of Loneliness*, Virago, 1982.)

H. G. Wells, in an article in the *Daily Herald*, attacked the Home Office for the seizure, and a few weeks later, the government began legal action against the book. Virginia Woolf and E. M. Forster, like others who may not have found the book to be the best-written thing in the world but supported its right to exist, sent a protest letter to the Home Secretary who had banned the book for its "distasteful subject."

"What," the letter asked, "of other subjects known to be more or less unpopular in Whitehall, such as birth control, suicide and pacifism? May we mention these? We await our instructions!" (Hermione Lee's *great* biography *Virginia Woolf, a Life*, Knopf, 1997.)

Virginia Woolf's *Orlando*, coyly subtitled "A Biography," was published by her own Hogarth Press in England on October 11, 1928. Dedicated to Vita Sackville-West, the book is about a time-traveling man who becomes a woman or woman who was once a man and his/her various love affairs. It is, as Woolf wrote to her lesbian paramour-dedicatee, "all about you and the lusts of your flesh and the lure of your mind." Their affair had begun in 1925. Vita, who sometimes referred to herself as Julian, often dressed, like her friend Radclyffe who called herself John, in male clothing.

A week and a half after the publication of *Orlando*, Woolf went to Cambridge with Sackville-West to deliver the talks on women and fiction that eventually developed into *A Room of One's Own*. Then on November 9, Woolf showed up at court to act as a witness on Hall's behalf, but was not called to testify.

Some things were becoming visible, but not everything. Some things took time.

The Well of Loneliness describes its hero/heroine, Stephen Gordon, as "grotesque and splendid, like some primitive thing conceived in a turbulent period of transition."

Radclyffe Hall wrote more books after *The Well of Loneliness* and hung out with writers and had a girlfriend and a life. (One of her pals and a literary mentor was Rebecca West, a one-time girlfriend of H. G. Wells.) But making visible what she did in 1928 remains what she is known for.

She/he/John/Radclyffe/Marguerite died in 1943, five years before the book for which she/John is most remembered was published in her (his?) homeland. I guess by 1948 they'd found people to truly be afraid of.

Is that progress? The movement from fearing what we shouldn't to what we should? From seeing what we haven't to what we must?

I first read Radclyffe Hall on the sly. I was studying Literature with a capital "L" in grad school, but that did not include, at the time, a writer like Radclyffe Hall.

One of the ways I supported myself then was working in a used bookstore. The guy who owned the store was bald and had a wild gray beard that went down to the middle of his chest. He usually wore overalls without a shirt, unless he was wearing his full tux. In addition to the bookstore, which he lived above, he ran a ritzy restaurant rich people came to, a scuzzy nightclub he had to throw drunks out of, a carpentry business with his brother and a small drug business. He didn't have the bookstore to make money. He had the bookstore because he was crazy about great writing. I was crazy about great writing too, and that's why he liked me.

One of his favorite gestures was to spread his big, sweaty, muscly arms wide, as if to embrace most of the books in the store and say, "Crap, fucking crap." Although there were exceptions. Such as Shakespeare, about whom he'd growl, "That guy can fucking write a play." Or Malcolm Lowry, "That guy can fucking write a novel."

If what I was reading was crap, he'd tell me. But if it wasn't, like Kafka, he'd mumble something like "that pansy" and then go into some long thing about Kafka and the central European artistic tradition and Jewish mysticism and the Kabbalah and the diaries and letters to Felice and I'd learn more in ten minutes of his ranting as he was tramping up the stairs to change out of his stinking overalls than I had learned in a week of class.

This was in Virginia in the '70s. Women had been admitted to the previously all-male university just the decade before and Blacks—the word was not yet "African American"—were beginning to get jobs as professors instead of only as custodians or maids. Things moved especially slowly for gays. Most people hadn't even heard of the Stonewall riots. Those of us who had were on the lookout for one another.

So it made a big impression on me one day when two girls, one of whom was very cute, came in the bookstore. They glanced furtively around to make sure there was no one else in hearing distance. Then the cute one asked, in a voice just above a whisper, if we had a copy of *The Well of Loneliness*. I sat up. I didn't know if we did, but I knew what she was asking for and it wasn't just a book "Oh," I said coolly, "Radclyffe Hall." They blushed because this showed them that I knew they meant the Lesbian Book. "I don't know if we have it. Check in the back," and I pointed there. They giggled and skittered off together.

I don't remember if they found the book. I do remember several months later, when I saw the cute one at the Gay Student Union dance,

I was not surprised. She was by herself and I asked her to dance. She had broken up with the other one and we danced the night away, etc.

Radclyffe Hall's *The Well of Loneliness* was not a book I would have asked my bookstore boss about. I had started reading it when we were getting way into High Modernism in class, so I snottily found it obvious, simplistic, maudlin, or in the words of my boss, "crap, fucking crap." The "Bible of Lesbianism," I was mortified to discover, was written in fairly awful prose. Now that I am older and a bit less of a snob, I see that despite Hall's pedestrian and utterly mainstream prose, her book was, as it remains, both brave and—something all too rare in art—important.

The Well of Loneliness was a sign, the one title those girls in the bookstore—who I later learned had been cruising me for weeks—knew that if they asked me about, my reaction would reveal if I was gay. Anyone could read other lesbian writers like Stein or Barnes or Woolf because those writers could "fucking write." But you didn't read Radclyffe Hall unless you were a dyke.

Here's how the jacket flap of my copy, a reissue made from the original 1928 plates, describes it:

> *The Well of Loneliness* presents the life story of Stephen Gordon, only child of Sir Philip and Lady Anna Gordon, who ardently desired a son in her place. How this circumstance influenced a natural tendency towards masculinity in Stephen Gordon, her tortured adolescence and her gradual development into maturity in this deviated direction, with all its tragic implications, is the theme of this book.

There were lots of things in this description that made a self-important English Lit grad student like me bristle. For starters, the name Stephen Gordon suggests a lineage with both the first Christian martyr, Stephen, a beautiful boy who was stoned to death, and the ultra-Romantic hero, George Gordon, Lord Byron who, adored as he was by swooning females, also had a thing for young men. In short, the name of the protagonist of *The Well of Loneliness* seemed both presumptuous and hokey. Secondly, the stereotype of the homosexual being "tortured" and "tragic" was just the kind of thing we were trying to work against in the '70s and '80s. But as I see it now, both the name and the fate of Hall's character were pretty forward-looking.

Prior to Radclyffe Hall, there had been literary portrayals of characters, mostly male and epitomized by the wealthy aesthete in Huysman's 1884 *Au Rebours*, the title of which is often translated *Against Nature*, whose aesthetics hinted at a shadowy, pathological demimonde of sexual decay. These fin de siècle novels did not ask for mainstream acceptance, much less sympathy, for these characters, but *The Well of Loneliness* did. Stephen Gordon was portrayed openly, in the language of the sexologists of the day, as an "invert." Hall's portrayal suggested that Gordon's "inversion" resulted from a genetic predisposition, not a condition to be cured or eradicated. Though the idea of the homosexual as tragic figure doomed to suffer may seem pathetic to modern queers, it was an important step in the development of gay identities.

In the '70s and '80s it was common to look down on Hall. During the women's movement, the last thing radical lesbians and feminists wanted was to be "masculine." If you chose a new name to replace the one your parents gave you, it should be something like Jasmine or Ruthdaughter or June Bloodmoon, not a guy's name like Stephen or John. You didn't want people to see you as mannish, but as a "woman-identified woman." But of course back then few people saw you at all.

In Wells's *The Invisible Man*, the problem is that after Griffin becomes invisible he can't get visible again. He gets kicked out of where he lives and he escapes to an inn in the countryside where he tries to concoct an antidote for his condition. Eventually he runs out of money, steals from people and breaks into the home of a Dr. Kemp. Kemp, hearing a commotion downstairs, goes to check and is stopped by an invisible hand. Here Griffin introduces, or rather reintroduces, himself to Kemp:

"I'm an invisible man ... And I want your help.... Don't you remember me, Kemp? Griffin, of University College? ... a younger student, almost an albino, six feet high, and broad, with a pink and white face and red eyes."

Most retellings of Wells's book skip over the fact that the man who becomes invisible by means of chemicals and the reversed refraction of light is albino, someone whose skin color already makes him, if not entirely invisible, at least disparaged and reviled.

Some people are just plain born like that, a way that others will not see or will not see as right, only as different, wrong, grotesque.

Maybe part of the reason the albino "stranger," as Griffin is called in the first sentence, becomes invisible is because when he had been visible people looked away from him, repulsed and fearful, or they stared, repulsed and fascinated, and after a while he just got fucking sick of it.

At the end of Wells's book, the Invisible Man is bashed to death by a gang of "normal" men.

This is the description of the dead man's body, now visible again:

> There lay, naked and pitiful on the ground, the bruised and broken body of a young man about thirty. His hair and beard were white,—not gray with age, but white with the whiteness of albinisms, and his eyes were like garnets.

He was old before his time, poor guy. He never had a chance.

In James Whale's movie, Griffin (Claude Raines) is a man who wants to do something great partly because he is a scientist but also to impress his girlfriend. Griffin figures out how to make himself invisible, but not how to make himself visible again. He doesn't realize, until too late, that staying invisible too long will drive one nuts. So he goes nuts.

The police find the Invisible One hiding in an old barn and set the barn on fire to smoke him out. It's snowing so when the barn goes up in flames and the Invisible Man runs out, everyone can see his footsteps. They catch him and shoot him but he doesn't die immediately so there can be a death scene with the girlfriend in the hospital.

The girlfriend sits at the side of the hospital bed. We cannot see the invisible boyfriend, of course, only that the sheets are shaped as if they are draped over a body. There's also that depression in the pillow like someone's head. As Griffin dies, he returns to visibility. We see, kind of like an X-ray (invented in 1893, two years before the book came out!) first the bones, then veins, the sockets of his eyes. Then eyes, then finally, skin.

You only see him fully when he's dead.

But then the Invisible Man gets to live again! *The Invisible Man Returns* stars Vincent Price, and was released in January 1940. Here's the plot: Sir (he's come up in the world) Geoffrey Radcliffe (Price) is sentenced to death, although he didn't do it, for the murder of his brother. But Dr. Frank Griffin, the brother of the original Invisible Man, goes to the prison where Price is being held before his execution. Dr. Griffin injects him with an invisibility drug that allows Radcliffe to escape. Radcliffe meets his loyal, waiting girlfriend at a hideaway. Willie Spears (Alan Napier, later Batman's butler on TV) reveals, under duress, that Cecil Hardwicke, the manager of the mining operation the Radcliffes run, committed the murder. The invisible Radcliffe chases Hardwicke who accidentally dies in a coal wagon. Radcliffe is hit by a stray bullet and nearly dies. Dr. Griffin gives Radcliffe a blood transfusion that not only keeps him from dying but also makes him visible again.

Vincent Price's face was only in the film for a few minutes. For most of the movie he only appeared, like Claude Raines before him, as a disembodied voice, like the disembodied voice of Agnes Nicholls who, around the time that Wells was dreaming up his book, brought forth in the adolescent Radclyffe Hall (still Marguerite at that point) the love that she would be encouraged to keep unseen until she wrote her famous book.

The Invisible Man Returns was released twelve years after the 1928 obscenity trial for *The Well of Loneliness*. Early in the movie there is a scene at the gate of the home of the Radcliffe clan: Radcliffe Manor. As if asking, Radcliffe (Radclyffe)—Man/or something else? Not a woman, exactly—but what? A she? A he?

The Radcliffe homestead gate was not the only one to ask Man

Or? about a female writer. While genteel "bluestocking" scribes of light poetry or romance were allowed to exist and practice the "lesser" or feminine genres, Radclyffe Hall and female writers who were not "genteel" were suspect, intellectuality being a bad thing in a woman, a form of brain sickness that led to their (our) being, in the words of Norman Mailer, "dyke-ily psychotic." (May he burn in hell.)

But other guys were not so threatened, including the hardly feminist Alfred Hitchcock. A couple of decades before Mailer, *Suspicion* (1941, Cary Grant, wonderful as ever; Joan Fontaine as irritatingly wimpy as ever), had room for a perfectly unmonstrous female writer, the mystery scribe Isobel Sedbuck (played by Auriol Lee) and her anonymous mannish female friend in Radclyffe Hall drag (cropped hair, jacket, shirt and tie), and played by some anonymous personage not listed in the credits, who pours the wine and guy-to-guy-ishly calls the Cary Grant character "chap." This woman writer and her man/or something "friend" aren't monsters, they're just a pair of colorful English eccentrics.

Was Radclyffe Hall a man/or something else unseen before? Who sees us when we are not seen? Who would be seen but isn't? "Things are because we see them," Wilde said. "And what we see and how we see it," he continued, "depend on the arts that have influenced us. To look at a thing is very different from seeing a thing. One does not see anything until one sees its beauty. Then, and then only, does it come into existence."

Would you see her without her shirt and tie? Or him without his yellow or green carnation? Maybe there a reason they're so "flamboyant." As if they'd not be seen if they were not.

The Invisible Man Returns includes a scene in which the invisible Vincent Price jokingly asks the girl he loves, "What does it feel like to have a phantom fiancee?" Which I guess is what you are if you can only have a phantom (read: second-class partnership) marriage.

I don't remember what the poor girl said.

7 One cannot hear the words "invisible" and "man" together with-

out thinking of Ralph Ellison's *Invisible Man* (1954), one of the great American novels of the 20th century. It begins:

> I am an invisible man. No, I am not a spook like those who haunted Edgar Allan Poe, nor am I one of your Hollywood-movie ectoplasms.... [For Hollywood ectoplasms see above.] My invisibility [is not] exactly a matter of biochemical accident to my epidermis. That invisibility to which I refer occurs because of a peculiar disposition of the eye of those with whom I come in contact. A matter of the construction of their inner eyes, those eyes with which they look through their physical eyes upon reality. I am not complaining, nor am I protesting either.

I am of course complaining and protesting both. I mean, People! How many times do we have to go through this invisibilizing of others? When are we vermin going to get that we're all here, we're all queer (or colored or weird or different) and just get used to it?

Ralph Ellison went to the Alabama Tuskegee Institute in 1933, where he became a clerk in the library and discovered Stein, Joyce, et al. His "aesthete" teacher Morteza Drezel introduced Ellison to Hardy's *Jude the Obscene*, I mean, *Obscure*. Ellison felt an affinity with the book's wounded, unseen, disparaged-by-others hero.

The first scene in *Invisible Man* recounts how a female object, an as-it-were invisible woman, is placed in front of several Negro men by white men to "prove" the lower animal nature of . . . of . . . uh . . . whom?

Them?

Whoever them is. Us?

Whoever it is who refused to see the human in front of one's very particular eyes.

Who is it we're not seeing now?

Who will not look or see?

Who else will we forget

and make invisible?

"Oh darn!" (See note 1 above.)

Moonlight, in a familiar room, falling so white upon the carpet, and showcasing all its figures so distinctly,—making every object so minutely visible, yet so unlike a morning or noontide visibility,—is a medium the most suitable for a romance-writer to get acquainted with his illusive guests. . . . Ghosts might enter here, without affrighting us. It would be too much in keeping with the scene to excite surprise, were we to look about us and discover a form beloved, but gone hence, now sitting quietly in a streak of this magic moonshine, with an aspect that would make us doubt whether it had returned from afar, or had never once stirred from our fireside.

—Nathaniel Hawthorne, "The Custom House,"
Preface to The Scarlet Letter

My Western

If only I'd known what to look for.
   If only I'd known how to read the writing on the screen.
   A private meaning just for me
   but I was looking wrong.

Then he was gone.

This is how the movie ends, the scene we won't forget: The child is facing away from us and watching someone leaving. "And mother wants you! I know she does!" the child shouts. "Come back!" But the man does not. "Come back!" the child shouts again, "Shane, come back!"
   Come back come back come back.
   My father can't come back because he's dead, and no one's really sure about the lone man on the horse. He came from far away and then he left.

He looked, far away, like a silhouette, first black and white, then color. Although the book said he was dark, in the movie he is blonde, as is the kid, who could have been his child and wished he was, though he already had a father.[1] The kid was looking out, before the stranger came, at a deer he wanted to shoot, except his rifle had no bullets. (His mother hated guns.) The kid was also looking up at the Wyoming sky—it's 1889—as wide and high and blue and vast as anything we've ever, ever seen or ever will. There are mountains too, both far away and crisp and cold, but also close, like everything. The kid is looking out at them and at the giant, lonely world.

Does everybody always want to be somebody else?

At first they wanted Montgomery Clift for Shane, but he was "not available," like what they say about the kind of men who can't make commitments (why don't they just say what they fucking mean?), so they got Alan Ladd and now no one can imagine Shane as anybody else.[2]

As if the way it ended was the only way it could.

At first they wanted William Holden for the father, but he was also "not available," so they got Van Heflin. Van Heflin was part Irish, born in Oklahoma, went to O.U. and was a navy man. All of these are exactly like my father.

They tried to get it right but you can't get everything. Some things they did but others not, you have to read between the lines, I mean the frames, or put in things you might not see but know are there because it all was there, if you knew how to look, if you looked right. Then you could see the way it was or it would be. It tried to tell you, and it was not what you thought.

At first they wanted Katherine Hepburn for the mother, but she was also "not available," so they got Jean Arthur. Jean Arthur, like my mother, once lived in Jacksonville, Florida. We all did when my father was stationed at Pensacola. This was a good posting, at least for me, because it meant he got to be mostly at home as opposed to away on a naval carrier when we might not see him for months. He was a pilot for the navy, though we did not know where he flew, and a photographer. My mother taught grade school in Florida, having given up her college dream of acting.

They brought Jean Arthur (who named herself after two of my favorite childhood heroes too, Jean (Joan) of Arc and King Arthur) out of retirement for it. She was 53 by then, eight years older than Van Heflin, and long past her heyday as a screwball comic. In her prime she'd also had a few romantic roles, including once as Cary Grant's love interest in *Only Angels Have Wings* (Howard Hawks, 1939), where she falls in love with the dashing pilot Cary Grant the way my mother fell in love with my dashing pilot father. My mother always referred to Cary Grant as "the world's most perfect man," and though Cary leaves Jean, it's only for a while because later he comes back.

My father didn't.

("Come back! Come back! Come back!")

Brandon De Wilde played the kid. He was blonde and fair and small, like Shane and me and my dad. Actually my father wasn't short, he was 5'10" or so, but built compact and wiry like Shane. Brandon de Wilde also had severely deep-set eyes that looked a little weird. I had, if not exactly the same thing, at least a "lazy eye" that had to be corrected with a patch. At first I hated it. I hated looking weird with the weird eye, then the weird patch, but then I liked the patch because it showed I was a cowgirl and I'd lost my eye in a fight. Or at the Alamo (*The Alamo*, John Wayne, 1960, starring himself), where I almost died while defending it with Davy Crockett.[3] Or to an Indian—not a nice, wise one, I was friends with them—an Apache or Comanche who had shot me in the eyeball with an arrow that I had to pull out myself.

I could have done Brandon de Wilde's part. Why didn't they pick me? True, I wasn't born till five years after they made it, and I was a girl, but they had already changed the name of the kid from Bob in the book to Joe in the movie, so why couldn't they also change Bob into a girl? I could have played that part. I could have done it better. I could have said "Come back! Come back!" so wonderfully he'd have had to.

Van Heflin invites Shane to dinner. Mom dresses up, sets the table for four and makes a special apple pie for the occasion. After dinner, Shane helps Dad remove a stump from the yard. The men decide he'll stick around to help the family on the farm. Shane becomes part of this nice domestic farmer's life as, around the valley, ranchers grumble about "sodbusters" fencing the range. After he's been at their home a while, little Joey asks the gunman to teach him how to shoot. He hesitates, then takes the kid to the corral and is showing him how to hold a gun when Mom comes out and stops them. She doesn't want her child to play with guns.

My father taught me how to shoot. He took me to the range where he practiced shooting "skeet" or "trap," clay pigeons, not something I could, with a bungled shot, maim, hurt or cause to suffer. I remember him telling me to squeeze the trigger evenly—don't jerk it—and always aim a bit in front of a moving target. I remember the weight of the gun in my arms, the cool of the metal, the buck of the blast, my shoulder sore for days.

Later he took me duck hunting. I wore my brother's hand-me-downs—a corduroy cap, the flaps folded down over my ears, too-big boots and camouflage pants and jacket. We were in a brown field and the air was cold and the sun was coming up. There was the sound of mens' and boys' and my boots on the crunchy, almost frozen ground, and also the sounds of calls and cries, the whup of wings because the ducks knew what was up. This was in Spain, where we were posted after Florida.

I think I remember this, but maybe I don't. Maybe I only think I do because I saw a photograph of me in such a field on such a day, holding my father's gun. I must have been 8 or 9 because the gun was about my height. I do not remember firing a gun on this or any other trip at any living thing, although I'm sure I begged my father to.

Did my mother see to that?

After he retired from the navy, Van Heflin had a successful career in the movies. After my father was piped over from the navy, he kind of went to hell.

Van Heflin did, however, play a failure in his last major role, which was in *Airport* (George Seaton, 1970). He played a husband who tries to blow himself up so his wife can get the insurance money. So, a heroic failure then. Whereas my father just plain old died of "natural causes."

They scattered his ashes at sea.

(Van Heflin's and my father's.)

Shane gets wounded in a gunfight. Shot in the gut in the saloon in town by the bad ranchers who are mean to good farmers like Van Heflin. Van Heflin had planned to go to fight them, but Shane, in a valiant and self-sacrificial move, socked him good so he couldn't go because if Shane got hurt by the bad guys, no big deal, but if the father got hurt, then who would take care of his wife and child?

Shane is not so wounded, however, that he can't come back to the farm after the fight to play the poignant scene we want to see. He looks down at the kid and the kid looks up at him and there's all of that "Come back! Come back!" etc.

I don't remember when my father left. He was away "on tour" with the navy most of the time I was a kid. Then after he was piped over and got civilian jobs, he traveled a lot. Then after he lost those jobs he stayed away for other reasons. So when it became official, through their divorce, that he was really leaving, it was like he already had. There was not any specific time or scene in which he walked or drove away or rode out on a horse and then did not come back. There was no time that I or anyone yelled after him, "Come back! Come back! Come back!"

He was already gone.

What if, when Joey cried "Come back," Shane had? What if we saw his face close up, his sudden recognition, then his tenderness, and then he turned his horse and looked back at the child? The child brightens! Full of joy! But only for an instant because the guy's been wounded, after all, and on his face is not a shining, all-forgiving, all-forgetting smile. No—No—He turns back with a gasp, a gag, a gurgle in this throat and starts to fall. He's slipping in the saddle, back and stomach twisted. The child sees him fall, but only partly because his feet are in the stirrups so he's stuck half on, half off the horse, which might be funny somewhere else but isn't here. He's trying to right himself but can't. He's writhing like an insect, like a centipede, a worm—Wait. We can't do this to them.

Okay. Then how about this: Let's say he turns, but in this version his feet slip out of the stirrups so he can actually fall all the way off the horse and into the child's arms. The child catches him, holds him. The wounded man's bent over now, exactly the height of the child, which might seem nice at first but isn't because now the child can see, close up, at eye level, in garish, gruesome Technicolor, the man's blown-apart skin and his guts gouging out and brown stuff and red stuff and oozy stuff. This wasn't in the script. This isn't stuff a child should see. The dying man is trying to hold or push his guts back in but they keep oozing through his fingers and over the tops of his hands. Now his face is moving, he's sputtering, gagging, trying to tell the child something. His mouth falls opens and he makes these bubbly hacking awful noises and blood starts burbling up then, shooting out of him, red at first, little splatters like drops of rain, big thick lines of it, then clots, black, viscous, thick and then a great big glob of it that splatters against the child's face.

The kid is so fucking terrified that it can hardly breathe.

The guy makes another gurgly noise and his face goes white and his eyes roll back in his head and he shivers like he's got the D.T.'s. He clenches, falls. The child holds him up.

How long does the child hold the man?

How long will this go on?

Is this why Shane did not come back?

Is this what his departure spared the child?

For a while my mother wanted to be an actress. She got away from Oklahoma, where she, like everyone else in my family except me, was born, to study speech and drama at Sophie Newcomb Women's College in New Orleans. She performed in plays (the screwball gal? romantic lead?) and studied radio during an era when such a study could have led her to the movies. But she suddenly returned to

Oklahoma. I don't know why. Is the answer in a scene that was deleted? An outtake on the cutting room floor?

After my mother returned to Oklahoma, she transferred to O.U. where, through his younger brother, Stanley, whom she was dating, she met my father.

Kind of like how Hallie does in *The Man Who Shot Liberty Valance* (John Ford, 1962). Hallie (Vera Miles) is a nice girl, the illiterate daughter (unlike my mom who loved to read) of the immigrant couple (isn't everyone white in America some kind of immigrant?) that runs the local canteen. At the start of the movie, she's sweet on handsome, swaggering, gun-toting Tom Doniphon (John Wayne). They're not exactly engaged, but everyone assumes she's promised to him. Then slender, earnest, Ransom Stoddard (James Stewart), a vest-wearing guy whose head is always in a law book, comes to town. Ransom is beaten up by the Liberty Valance gang and John Wayne rescues him. The two become friends and John treats the gentle, bookish guy the way an older boy might treat his little brother. He calls him "Pilgrim" meaning "greenhorn" because he thinks he'll always be his sidekick.

My father called my Uncle Stanley "Little Brother" all their lives.

Uncle Stanley told me once that he remembered their father coming home from World War I and teaching him and his big brother how to take apart and clean and put a gun back together, then how to shoot it. My father was better at this than Stan. Stan's pursuits were quieter; next to his confident older brother he was shy.

What my father remembered about his father was how he was henpecked by his wife.[4] She ran away to New York once (to be an actress?). My father remembered his father washing dishes at the kitchen sink, a hero and a veteran diminished by his wife.

John Wayne was not John Wayne until the movies.

His name at birth was, after his Irish mother, Marion. Marion Robert Morrison. Needless to say, he wanted a nickname. When he was a child, he went everywhere with his dog, a huge thing named Duke. People started calling the boy "Little Duke." When he got older it became just "Duke."

He kept that name and got another when he started playing heroes in the movies.

My father's name was Vergil (spelled with an "e" not an "i" like Dante's guide) Neal Brown, Jr. after his Irish father. He hated the name and he swore he'd never name a child that. When he was a kid they called him "Hershey." I don't know why because I never asked. What else did I not ask about? What else did I not think about until it was too late?

Perhaps the first kind thing my father did for his son was to name him plain old Bill.

Everyone else, besides John Wayne, calls Jimmy Stewart "Rance." Because he helps out in the kitchen, wears an apron, likes to read and is terrible with guns, they treat him like he isn't quite a man. Though Rance is grateful for John Wayne's help, he wants to fight his own battles and turn the gun-happy wild West into a law-abiding state. Rance doesn't want to carry a gun, but John insists, for his own safety, that he learn to shoot. He tries to teach him but he's a miserable shot, so when the evil Liberty Valance (a leather-clad, whip-toting Lee Marvin) challenges Ransom to a gunfight, John has to rescue Rance a second time.

As Jimmy is about to fire, John, hidden in the shadows, shoots Lee Marvin dead. Unaware of who really killed Valance, gun-shy Stoddard Ransom becomes famous as the man who shot Liberty Valance, and, riding this law-and-order reputation, is elected representative at the territorial convention. After Stewart is voted in, John Wayne tells him that it was he, not him, who shot him.

Jimmy Stewart feels awful that he's been given credit for something he didn't do, but he's already made a commitment to the convention. Drunken, angry John tells Jimmy not to tell because the people need to believe in something. Rance goes to Washington and is eventually elected senator. He also marries Hallie.

Which brings us back to my parents. Hallie starts out with the bigger, charismatic guy who's going to turn out bad and switches to, then marries, his less-showy greenhorn sidekick who is going to turn out good. This is the opposite of my mom, who started out with the less-showy guy who is going to turn out good (Uncle Stanley), then switched to, then married, the older, charismatic one, who kind of went to hell, my dad.

When Tom sees Hallie taking care of the traumatized Pilgrim after the shootout with Lee Marvin, Tom thinks she's sweet on Rance. Tom freaks out, drinks too much, burns down the house and basically, for the rest of his life, kind of goes to hell. In the movie he falls apart because he loses the girl. But my father didn't lose the girl, so why'd he fall apart? Uncle Stanley married, had kids, kept a job, did not become a boozer.

After John goes to hell, the only person who can stand to be around him is loyal Pompey (Woody Strode), a former slave.

It was the early '60s when we lived in Florida. Years later, my mother told me about how, when she was teaching there, some white parents wouldn't *ever* let their kids be absent from school because then enrollment would go down and the school would have to integrate. These white parents would send their kids to school even when they were really sick with things like impetigo. I don't remember this, although I do remember—and it's one of my most shameful memories—preschool me, after one of my father's friends had come over to our house to visit, referring to his friend with the "N" word. My father firmly, carefully, quietly told me to never, ever use that word again and why. My father may have been a troubled man, but he was right about a few important things.[5]

The Man Who Shot Liberty Valance is a frame narrative. It starts with the senator and his wife returning to a little town to mourn the passing of some old drunk. When local newsmen ask the senator why he has come back to mourn the dead guy, he tells, at last, the story of who really shot Liberty Valance. He wants the paper to print this story and finally honor the man who'd done such a heroic deed back when. The editor refuses. "This is the West, sir," he tells the senator, "When the legend becomes fact, print the legend."

Tom Doniphon had never told anyone else about who really shot Liberty Valance, and he suffered for that. Is that what happens to the guy who knows the truth but has to keep it secret? Was this the real reason Tom Doniphon went to hell?

Some things about John Wayne:
John Wayne hated his birth name.
John Wayne never actually fought in a World War, but he loved the military. John Wayne was very pro-gun.
John Wayne was asked to be George Wallace's running mate when Wallace ran for governor of Alabama. He turned them down so they got Lester Maddox.
John Wayne was married three times.
John Wayne smoked packs and packs of cigarettes a day.

John Wayne got cancer.
John Wayne died.

Some things about my father:
My father hated his birth name.
My father never actually fought in World War II, but he loved
    the military. My father was very pro-gun.
My father went duck hunting once with Lester Maddox.
My father was married three times.
My father smoked packs and packs of cigarettes a day.
My father got cancer.
My father died.

Does everybody always want to be somebody else?
To be from some place they are not?
To always be arriving or departing?

Shane did not come back to Little Joey. But when Brandon de
Wilde grew up, he got to be John Wayne's son. It was, oddly enough,
not in a western but in a movie about World War II, *In Harm's Way*
(Otto Preminger, 1965). John Wayne is Rockwell Torrey, a navy officer who left his family years before because he couldn't be both a
family man and a navy man. Brandon de Wilde is an only child and, in
the way that can only happen in Hollywood, is stationed near his father, John Wayne. Exactly like in *Rio Grande* (John Ford, 1950) a son
whom he hasn't seen in fifteen years is stationed near his father, John
Wayne. This time, however, it's 1965 and although the war in Vietnam
isn't quite as hated as it's going to get, the son hates being in the navy.
He's only in it to eventually become a journalist or something, and

we already know from *Liberty Valance* how untrustworthy journalists are. But then Pearl Harbor happens and the son sees his father in his element and comes to understand, in a way I and my anti-Vietnam peacenik siblings never did, why a father has to leave his family. The son and father also double-date.

John Wayne's love interest is the no-nonsense nurse, Patricia Neal (Neal was my father's middle name!), who is roommates with a younger nurse who goes out once with Brandon de Wilde. Patricia Neal is also kind of the crush interest for modern cowboy Brandon de Wilde when he plays bad Paul Newman's shy, younger cousin in *Hud* (Martin Ritt, 1963).[6] (Is there some kind of Freudian thing going on here? The boy gets a crush on his father's girlfriend after she becomes his cousin's almost girlfriend?) Paul Newman is the bad cowboy—violent, yelling, crashing around drunk—who almost gets her but she gets away in time.

I never saw my father violent and I don't believe, at home, he ever was. My mother always said if he had ever laid a hand on any of us she would have left him in an instant, and I believe she would have.

But my sister, seven years older than me, remembers times when we were small and our mother, hearing our father outside, bustled the three of us to our room at the back of the house and told us to stay there no matter what happened. My sister had to keep us quiet as she listened to our father yell and the sounds of breaking things.

I don't remember any of this.

Come back come back come back!
No, don't. No. Please. Do not come back.

The movie *Shane* was adapted from a book by Jack Schaefer that begins "in the summer of '89," which was sort of the beginning of my family too. Eighteen eighty-nine was the year of one of the great Oklahoma land rushes. (See *Cimarron*, Charles Walters and Anthony Mann, 1960, for a version of April 22, 1889, when, at high noon, with a gunshot and a bugle call, some 50,000 people, most white, ran or-rode on horseback or in wagons or on trains to try to claim a piece of the two million acres the U.S. government was giving away, hav-ing wrested it with bullets, blood, etc., from the people who had lived there previously but were not white. This was the beginning of the state of Oklahoma.)[7] I don't know if anyone in my bloodline took part in this 1889 land rush, or snuck in earlier as Sooners. I do know that my maternal grandfather was born in Canadian County, Oklahoma Territory, one year after the land rush and my grandmother two years later in Blaine County, Oklahoma. Then, a generation or so later, my father and my mother and Van Heflin were born in Oklahoma City.

Does everybody always want another set of parents?
Does everybody always want to hear "Come back"?

I wasn't born in Oklahoma like everyone else in my family. I was born in California when my dad was stationed there, but I was the kid who really loved the West. I wanted, longer than most kids do, to be a cowboy or cowgirl. The important thing was the riding and shooting and being free. We lived in Spain in the mid-sixties, the era of the great TV westerns, so we didn't get to see them first-run, but *Bonanza* was so famous that they dubbed it into Spanish. I remember a story from that time about my father going drinking with Dan Blocker (Hoss). My father came home and told us that Dan Blocker was a very, very huge man and he could really hold his drink. I couldn't believe my father had met Dan Blocker and hung out with him. I was thrilled. I couldn't keep my mouth shut. I told everyone.

John Wayne's last movie was *The Shootist* (Don Siegel, 1976). It begins with a bunch of old black-and-white clips of early John Wayne movies. We see the young man—handsome, clear-eyed, confident—ride and shoot his way through the ranges and mesas, canyons and plateaus of the classic West, a stranger or a loner or a soldier who will save us. Then we see him age—his suntanned face gets wrinkled and his girth expands. His walk becomes more measured, slow. By the time the black-and-white runs out, he's old.

He rides into a town—buggies in the background, a primitive streetcar—and buys a newspaper that announces the death of Queen Victoria. It's 1901, the end of an era of history and the beginning of the end of this man's life. John Books has traveled for days to see the one doctor he can trust, a man he knew when they were young, James Stewart. Doc Stewart, no longer a greenhorn like Rance Stoddard was, tells John that the pain in his lower back is cancer and that he's going to die of it.

"How bad is it going to be?" the old man asks, and Doc tells him he doesn't want to know.

But John insists, so James tells him it's going to be bad, very bad, and gives him a bottle to take a nip of whenever he needs it, the way my father carried a flask. Assuming a false identity, John rents a room in Widow Rogers's house, where he expects to die. Widow Rogers is actually Lauren Bacall, who had lost her husband, Humphrey Bogart, to cancer in '57. She's a single mom with a now fatherless only child played by, not Brandon de Wilde, who is dead, but Oklahoma-born Ron Howard. Ron Howard's name is "Gillom," a name I'd never heard before, which is perhaps why I first heard it as "William," like my brother, who was often called "Guillermo" when we lived in Spain or Texas near the border.

Gillom learns that his mother's boarder is the notorious gunman John Books. He is so thrilled he can't keep his mouth shut and he tells everyone. In a familiar rite of passage scene, the kid asks the man to teach him how to shoot. Gillom is a better shot than Jimmy Stewart was back when the place was still a territory, and the teacher has grown up too. He's older and wiser, recites his cowboy code of honor and tells young Gillom that shooting is less about your technique than your mental state. Then they go and blast the hell out of some targets.

The Shootist ends when John Wayne, after bidding a poignant farewell to the Widow Bogart, goes to the saloon to confront the trio of outlaws he's arranged to meet there. Then, rather than from the filthy, slow and long decay of cancer, he goes down in a blaze of bullets, taking all the bad guys with him. Gillom sees this scene and we know he will tell of it (his future as a movie director is just around the corner), so John Books will not suffer, as Tom Doniphon did, by having his heroic deed kept a secret.

John Wayne died three years later. (Cancer).

Brandon de Wilde was already dead (a motorbike, a rainy road) and so was Alan Ladd. The man whose nickname had been "Tiny" as a kid (he hated that) finally went down, at age 50, with an overdose of booze and pills, an "accident" like Hemingway's. He'd also tried to shoot himself before, just ten years after *Shane*, which was ironic considering that during the filming of *Shane* he was so gun-shy they had to do more than 100 takes of the scene of him trying to teach the kid to shoot.

The mom and dad, Van Heflin and Jean Arthur, died, peacefully, of heart attacks.

My father outlived all of them.

My brother told me recently our father had a secret.[8]

Our father said, years afterward, that when we lived in Florida, he'd flown a mission over Cuba and was chased by Russian planes. I don't know if my father fired back. I know, because my brother told me, that our father had been sworn to never tell.

My brother had not thought much of this—our father had told us many things when he was in his cups—until he saw a movie.

Thirteen Days (Roger Dolandson, 2000), based on a true story, begins with a series of aerial photos. A nameless military pilot flying over Cuba has found something that looks to him like a missile build-up. It's October 1962, and J.F.K. is in the White House. (My father always hated J.F.K.) The military brass tells J.F.K. they think the Soviets are planning to place missiles in Cuba that can hit the United States. Having recently come off the Bay of Pigs mess, Kennedy is skeptical about his generals' interest in invading Cuba again. The president orders more flights, more photographs. Kevin Costner, J.F.K.'s second right-hand man after Bobby, makes personal phone calls to the pilots down in Florida to tell them that even if they are fired upon, they must not return fire because if they do, they'll start another war, which will be nuclear, and all of us will die.

The two pilots, also nameless, are shot at but they don't fire back. Or maybe there's only one pilot. And maybe he goes down? I can't remember, and besides, it's just a movie *based on* a true story, it didn't say it *was* a true story. In any event, they get more photos, then J.F.K. and Bobby and Kevin Costner stand up to the Russians and avert world war. Also, Bobby makes a deal under the table for us to get rid of some of our bases near Russia so they can save face, but all of this has got to be kept secret.

Was my father the one who took those pictures? Was he chased by a Russian plane and did he see his buddy die? Was he the shootist who did not shoot back?[9]

My father didn't like the West. He always called Oklahoma City the most godforsaken city on the planet. He only retired in Texas because he wanted to be near the Gulf (great fishing) and a navy base. He shopped at the PX until he died.

To my father, the term "cowboy" was an insult reserved for mannerless brutes, uneducated clods or rednecks singing twangy, unsophisticated ditties. He was more the nightclub or juke-joint type.

A few years before my father died, his wife (his third, already a widow when she married him) gave my father a Humphrey Bear-gart teddy bear, complete with raincoat and fedora. He pretended it was ridiculous but he loved it. It sat on the mantel over their fireplace in the den along with some of my father's German drinking mugs and photos of her grandkids and her kids.

My father did not go down in an airplane or in a blaze of bullets, but died of "natural causes," which, in his case, could have included lots of things. In the years before he died, he had been sick with slurry speech and memory loss, a stroke or two, blood pressure problems, too much booze, and, the thing that would have got John Books, the old man's illness, prostate cancer. If my father had lived long enough for his cancer to progress, I suspect he would have been, like John Books or Tom Doniphon, an awful patient. By dying before his cancer made him bedridden, he made it easier for everyone around him. Did my father somehow will himself to die so that his wife wouldn't have go through that? Was his death then, in his small way, heroic?

My father forbade his wife to have a funeral, but we wanted to remember him so we all flew down to see her and have a big meal, with a lot of booze, in our father's honor. We went around the table and said things we remembered. My brother couldn't say much without crying but finally he got out something about how our father, when he took him hunting, taught him to love the out-of-doors. I didn't have much to say from childhood, but I said how glad I was when Dad accepted my partner so lovingly when I took her to meet him.

My Western

At the start of *Shane*, the book, there is this dinner scene:

We sit down to supper and a good one. Mother's eyes . . . sparkled as our visitor kept pace with father and me. Then we . . . all leaned back and while I listened the talk ran on almost like . . . old friends around a familiar table, but I could sense that it . . . was following a pattern. Father was trying, with mother helping . . . and both of them avoiding direct questions, to get ahold of facts . . . about this Shane and he was dodging them at every turn. . . . He was . . . aware of their purpose and not in the least annoyed by it. He was mild and courteous and spoke readily enough. But always put . . . them off with words that gave no real information . . . no news . . . about himself. His past was fenced as tightly as our pasture. . . . All they could learn was that he was riding through.

A classic western sunset. A stranger on a horse is passing through. We fall in love. With him and with the stories we imagine he could tell but does not. We fill his secret past with our desires and the things we are afraid we cannot do. We do not want to know what he is not. The stories we will tell of him will save us from our lies.

I tried to see him everywhere
in places he was not
but didn't look in places he would be.
A stranger here from far away
forever coming back.

Rebecca Brown

NOTES

1 Jack Schaefer, *Shane*, (Houghton-Mifflin/Bantam, 1949).

2 Most of the stuff about the making of *Shane* comes from Michael F. Blake, *Code of Honor: The Making of Three Great American Westerns, High Noon, Shane and The Searchers*, (Taylor Trade Publishing, 2003). I have to confess I never saw this movie when I was a kid. I saw it the first time year or so ago. By then everybody was dead.

3 To shoot John Wayne's *The Alamo* they had to build a fake Alamo in a little town in Texas (Brackettville) that didn't really have much going on before the movie, though what town would with a name like that, like your whole existence was in brackets, like you were just an afterthought, a second-class or minor thing, a footnote? But then, after they made the fake Alamo in Brackettville, it became "Alamo Village," as if it was something from the olden days. It wasn't, but that didn't stop it from being used a million times after *The Alamo* as a movie set, thereby making the former nothing town a star of stage, screen and television.

The John Wayne material comes from *John Wayne: The Man Behind the Myth* by Michael Munn (New American Library, 2004) and from *John Wayne: American Legend* (produced by Van Ness Films/ A&E network, 1998), and from some of the 169 movies he made.

4 I'd never actually thought about the word "henpecked" until recently when Chris and I were taking a walk near her son's house outside Phoenix and came across a peacock farm. It was a poor farm—scrappy, dusty. You could tell it used to be out in the country but the suburbs had grown up around it. The peacocks were beautiful and strutting their amazing fantails. Then I saw a peahen come up to one of cocks and start pecking at its head. It pecked and pecked and pecked. The male's beautiful feathers went down and he made these pathetic squeaky noises and tried to skitter away from the female. The peahen was brown, dowdy, dusty-looking, as scrappy as the farm and stronger than the male. She chased him around and pecked at him, punishing him for something, for being beautiful maybe, and he couldn't fight back. He was, with all his pretty finery, useless. The hen was the power and the brains and she'd have had him by the balls if he had them.

My mother said about my father's mother: "She never washed a dish in her whole life." Her husband, my father's father, did the dishes. I have this image of him standing in an apron by the sink. I don't know if I ever actually saw that, or if that's just an impression I inherited.

My father had a terrible work ethic, never wanted to do anything around the house. I never saw him wash a dish, or even do men things like mow the lawn. Whenever my mother said anything about the lawn, my father said his back was acting up—some mysterious wound from "the war"—so, although he was able to go out hunting or fishing or ride around on his boat, one of us kids would have to go out and mow the lawn. I wonder if his father's being henpecked was a reason.

5 I remember, also shamefully, in junior high, going on a Girl Scout outing and being in the car with our leader and her saying, very primly, "Lock your doors, girls, we're going through Nigger Town!" and no one saying anything, just locking the doors and looking down into our laps mortified that anyone would hear her, or maybe worse, see that we were with her on an outing, i.e., that though we were in junior high, we were still in Girl Scouts. I also remember taking "care packages"—hand-me-down clothes and old toys—to people there before Christmas and being mortified that we'd recognize some of the black kids from school. There weren't many black kids in school so even if you didn't know them, you knew who they were if you saw them and they saw you, you both would have to admit that you knew where they lived and that they were poor and that you were a do-goodie church kid going around with do-goodie white church ladies and that even if you didn't call it that yourself, everyone called it "Nigger Town" and that you didn't do a thing at all about that.

6 Why couldn't I have had just some of what Brandon de Wilde got? Why didn't I get to meet Patricia Neal? I could have had a decent crush on her. Why didn't I get to meet the Beatles, like Brandon de Wilde did when he flew to the Bahamas when they were shooting *Help!* to bring them some pot? He can keep Gram Parsons and Emmylou Harris writing that song about him after he died, "In My Hour of Darkness" (from *Grievous Angel*, 1973). I recognize Parson's genius, of course, but I can actually kind or take or leave Emmylou Harris.

7 My grandmother had a kids' book she read to us from, about the western migrations. It had a picture on the cover of a Davy Crockett–type (bearskin hat) leading his women and children and wagons west, assisted by his faithful Indian (feather headdress) guide. My grandmother had written notes in this book about things her ancestors had done. I thought my mother got this book from her when she died, then I got it from her when she died, but I couldn't find it. So, for Oklahoma history I went, I admit, to Wikipedia, but I checked all external links. The best link was William Willard Howard, "The Rush to Oklahoma," *Harper's Weekly* 33 (May 18, 1889), John W. Reps, ed., Cornell University, http://www.library.cornell.edu/Reps/DOCS/landrush.htm.

I don't know who to ask anymore about where that book of my grandmother's might be because everyone is dead.

8 Our father had a secret that he told my brother, as opposed to a secret he didn't know although someone else knew it about him which is the kind of secret Van Heflin had. I found out about Van Heflin's secret in a book called *Eleanor's Rebellion*, by David Siff (Knopf, 2000), who, it turns out, was a son Van Heflin didn't know he had. Siff grew up to be an actor, and when he learned that the man he had always thought was his father was not his father, but Van Heflin was, he became obsessed with Van Heflin. Heflin was dead by then so the son wrote a book about it.

I wonder what it's like for a man who fathers a child but doesn't know it. Maybe the woman doesn't know who the father is or maybe she does but doesn't tell the guy. Does the guy know it somehow somewhere? In his innards? Or his DNA? A place beyond the things you can remember?

9 The pilots were unnamed in the movie, but it was easy enough for me to find their names—even in a kids' book (*The Cuban Missile Crisis*, by Catherine Hester Gow [Lucent Books, 1997], pg. 8). Neither name was Vergil Neal Brown, Jr.

Then I thought, so what if the book said guys named Major Richard Heyser and Major Rudolph Anderson, Jr. photographed surface-to-air missiles in Cuba on October 14, 1962? Maybe my dad shot photographs on other days. Maybe my dad flew on another day or several other days! Maybe my father was sent out as bait, to see if the Russkies would chase him and they did! Then maybe my father had to do amazing plane maneuvers that only he could do! Then, after he had tempted the Russkies out and been chased by them but escaped, then maybe my dad came back and reported in secret to J.F.K. and J.F.K. was chicken at first which was why my dad hated him but then when the other guys around J.F.K. realized, after my dad's report, exactly what we, the U.S.A. and the entire free world were dealing with, they decided what to do and then they did and they told my father to not tell *anyone*, *ever*, which he didn't until, years later he told my brother.

Or maybe they entirely made up the names Major Richard Heyser and Major Rudolph Anderson, Jr., who never existed at all, were only made-up names, invented to protect the real hero, a man who was as heroic as—no, more heroic than—John Wayne or Shane or anyone: my father, Lieutenant Commander Vergil Neal Brown, Jr., the man who had, secretly, and thereafter tormentedly because of secretly (would he have been better off if he had told?), saved the entire world.

In the old countries, with which fiction has long been conversant, a certain conventional privilege seems to be awarded to the romancer; his work is not put exactly side by side with nature; and he is allowed a license with regard to every-day probability in view to the improved effects which he is bound to produce thereby. Among ourselves, on the contrary, there is as yet no such Faery Land, so like the real world, that, in a suitable remoteness, one cannot well tell the difference, but with an atmosphere of strange enchantment, beheld through which the inhabitants have a propriety of their own. This atmosphere is what the American romancer needs.

—Nathaniel Hawthorne, *Preface to* The Blithedale Romance

Young Goodman Brown: A Gloss

Young Goodman Brown came forth at sunset into the street of Salem village; put his head back, after crossing the threshold, to exchange a parting kiss with his young wife. And Faith, as the wife was aptly named, thrust her own pretty head into the street, letting the wind play with the pink ribbons of her cap while she called to Goodman Brown.

"Dearest heart," whispered she, softly and rather sadly, when her lips were close to his ear, "prithee put off your journey until sunrise and sleep in your own bed to-night. A lone woman is troubled with such dreams and such thoughts that she's afeared of herself sometimes. Pray tarry with me this night, dear husband, of all nights of the year."

"My love and my Faith," replied young Goodman Brown, "of all nights in the year, this one night must I tarry away from thee. My journey, as thou callest it, forth and back again, must needs be done 'twixt now and sunrise. What, my sweet, pretty wife, dost thou doubt me already, and we but three months married?"

Rebecca Brown

"Then God bless you!" said Faith, with the pink ribbons;
"and may you find all well when you come back."[1]

Come back, come back, come back, you begged, but I would not.
You needed me and I had promised, when we wed, that I would stay,
but I did not. I went out on the journey I would keep apart from you.
I went out to the wilderness to meet with whom I once had sworn, as
on a child's grave, I never would.

Put off your journey, you begged again. You couldn't believe that I
would leave. But I'm not good at promises.

A lone woman is troubled with such dreams and such thoughts that
she's afeared of herself sometimes, you confessed.

I too had had such thoughts. They'd come to me unbidden, cold,
as if a scourge. I'd thought that when I married you, I would be saved
from them. But I was not. So I decided then instead of fighting I would
join. Our fearful dreams my father had had as well.

Pray tarry, you begged a final time.

I didn't.

I only walked alone a while, then I was joined by an old familiar,
a good man, like I'd told myself I seemed.

For few are ever as we seem. There was a thing inside of me that
recognized the thing inside of him. I did not turn, was not repulsed,
but followed him. We met the others in the dark and did what we do
not admit (the lashings, brandings, pressings under rocks, the drownings and the shacklings, the auction blocks and selling up the river,
the surveillance). I did these things my fathers did; I turned me into
them.[2]

When I came back, you said I'd changed. You sensed something was wrong with me, and when you asked, I lied.

I got away with lying for a while. I told you stories and made excuses and, because you were an innocent, at least back then, you believed me.

But then the more I went away on my dark, secret errands, the more I kept away from you, though I told sweeter, more outlandish lies in public, you stopped believing me.

You said I'd changed; I said I hadn't. I told you you were imagining things. You were a troubled woman, nervous, high-strung, tired. You needed sleep. Lie down and rest, I said. Lie down. Forget.

I kept you like a child and you went nuts. You tore your hair in public and repented loudly, often, confessing things you hadn't done, denying things you had. You wept and wailed, heard voices. You said you saw the future—the end was coming soon!—and you knew who was evil and was damned.

Should I have known that first night when I left, that if I left, when I returned you also would have changed?

I thought I'd get away with it, as if that first night would be the only one, just once.

But of course it wasn't only once.

It was the way I was.

Did part of you already know that then? That I would do forever things I'd lie about and make excuses for?

Does part of your hysteric doomsday rant make sense? That someday someone will dish to me what I dished out to them?

Rebecca Brown

I imagine someone *putting back my head*. I imagine my head is put back by a hand of a color not my own, a hand that holds a branding iron, the butt of gun, a fire hose, a noose.

Or maybe the putting back is a kind of mercy. A way to keep me from lying my way even deeper into the hole I have been digging for myself, to prevent me from telling yet again the same old trumped-up tale of my heroic errand to the wilderness (in which I brought items including, but not limited to, smallpox, deforestation, firearms, Coca-Cola, McDonald's, the obesity epidemic and the public confession of things that should be kept private [though actually had latter remained a simple, truthful story of mystery, gratitude and change, it might—and I mean *might*—have been okay, but I could not leave well enough alone and had to start sneaking in sly little digs about how the health and wealth with which I had been "blessed" was due not only to God but to me—my ingenuity and work ethic that was so different from that of the heathens who danced around lasciviously in their birthday suits and fornicated without the sanction of either my church or state, thereby turning public confession into either public condemnation of anyone not exactly like me, or, later, public competition with anyone who *was* like me. See Jerry Springer, et al.]) where I shouldn't have goddamn barged in in the first place.[3]

To think I truly once believed that I and mine could make a better, fairer world, where one could start or start again, as equal with one's fellow man (females not yet reading on our equality radar), as opposed to being held down by our old, selfish fathers.

Though almost as soon as I started here, I turned into them.

Perhaps, dear Faith, you know too well the evil I've become, while also you remember that the day we wed we made a vow to stay forever one. Maybe that's what's driven you insane. You're stuck with me. Now what?

We two *exchange a parting kiss.*

As if of peace? Forgivingly? As if bygones are gone? (Though they are not . . .) My kissing is a last resort, a play-pretend apology. Not for me (I'm not admitting anything), but for those far-off distant fathers of the past. I boo-hoo-hoo, "Oh, woe is them!" and "Wasn't all that too terrible!" as if it's nothing of my own, for history is over.

But the past is not so long ago, you tell me, and neither is the future.

You see the future, where, you say, someone or ones—the "darkies" or the hired help, the servant girls, the low—will stop me when I try to leave, demanding, because *all has not been found well,* that I clean up this mess. Then when I can't—and I will not be able to, it really is a very nasty mess—they'll have to do as I did them, whether shackles or drownings or brands or bombs, or pillory or trail of tears, or lynch mob or electroshock, my head put back, etc.

No story will undo my deeds. No words will make them stop.

I pray that you will not be there to see it.

NOTES

1 "Young Goodman Brown" was one of Hawthorne's earliest tales, first published in the *New England Magazine* in April 1835, and then included in *Mosses from an Old Manse* (1846).

We Browns go back a long way in this country, both in real life and fantasy, in stories that are told of us and those we tell ourselves and those we do not tell.

2 American mainstream culture derives from these sources: England (our official language and laws); race warfare (killing the Natives to take the land; building an entire economy on slave labor); and religious fanaticism (the Puritans and everything created in opposition to them, such rock 'n' roll, jazz, feminism, sex for anything other than babies); and the public confession by which we try to both explain everything and explain everything else away.

3 Regarding the retelling of old tales, the author of *Twice Told Tales* (1837) had this to say (in *A Wonder-Book for Girls and Boys*, 1852) about that:

> It will be observed by everyone who attempts to render these legends malleable in his intellectual furnace, that they are marvelously independent of all temporary modes and circumstances. They remain essentially the same, after changes that would affect the identity of almost anything else.
>
> [The author] does not therefore plead guilty to a sacrilege, in having sometimes shaped anew, as his fancy dictated, the forms that have been hallowed by . . . antiquity. . . . No epoch of time can claim a copyright on these immortal fables . . . . they are legitimate subjects for every age to clothe

with its own garniture of manner and sentiment, and to im-
bue with its own morality.
(pp. v–vi, *A Wonder-Book for Girls and Boys*, Grosset &
Dunlap, 1967)

I rest my case.